C0061 62374

D0358185

Gla:
Libr.
nam

First published in the UK in 2016 by
Apple Press
74–77 White Lion Street
London N1 9PF
United Kingdom

www.apple-press.com

Copyright © 2016 Quantum Books Ltd.

All rights reserved. No part of this publication may be
reproduced, stored in a retrieval system or transmitted in any
form or by any means, electronic, mechanical, photocopying,
recording, or otherwise, without the written permission of the
copyright holder.

ISBN 9781845436353

Printed in China by Shanghai Offset Printing Products Ltd
9 8 7 6 5 4 3 2 1

This book was conceived, designed and produced by
Quantum Books Limited
6 Blundell Street
London N7 9BH
United Kingdom

Publisher: Kerry Enzor
Project Editors: Charlotte Frost and Lucy Kingett
Editorial Assistant: Emma Harverson
Production Manager: Zarni Win
Designer: Lucy Parissi
Food Styling by Jassy Davis
Photography by Simon Pask

Glasgow Life Glasgow Libraries	
W	
C 006162374	
Askews & Holts	10-Feb-2016
641.65347 FD	£14.99

WE LOVE KALE

Over 100 Delicious & Healthy
Hand-Picked Recipes

KRISTEN BEDDARD, KAREN S. BURNS-BOOTH, CAROLYN COPE,
JASSY DAVIS & KRISTINA SLOGGETT

APPLE

CONTENTS

22

32

35

52

57

58

68

79

85

MAIN COURSES

SOUPS, SALADS & SIDES

BAKES & DESSERTS

KEY TO SYMBOLS

- (V) VEGETARIAN
- (VG) VEGAN (AND VEGETARIAN)
- (DF) DAIRY-FREE
- (GF) GLUTEN-FREE
- (WF) WHEAT-FREE

Vegetarian and vegan recipes are tagged at the top of the pages showing main recipes.

91

97

126

141

142

148

156

161

167

MEET THE BLOGGERS

KRISTEN BEDDARD is the American founder of Paris-based **The Kale Project** and blog, a highly successful initiative to reintroduce kale to France. Through her work with local French farmers, *le chou kale* can now be found at various outdoor markets and supermarkets. Kristen currently resides in Paris.

KAREN S. BURNS-BOOTH is a professional recipe writer and food stylist who splits her time between the UK and France. In addition to writing for her own site, **Lavender and Lovage**, she regularly contributes to a variety of print publications, and creates recipes for major brands in the UK and Europe.

CAROLYN COPE is a food and lifestyle writer and the voice behind the popular blog **Umami Girl**, where the world is equal parts eat-to-live and live-to-eat. An avid traveller, musician and yogi, she is based in greater New York City, USA.

JASSY DAVIS is a London-based recipe writer for British organic vegetable company Abel & Cole and a professional food stylist. Her recipes in this book are inspired by Asian flavours and world food. Her blog is **Gin and Crumpets**.

KRISTINA SLOGGETT is a vegan health-food writer and recipe developer. Her blog **spabettie** focuses on plant-based recipes with vibrant colours and bright flavours for the vegan community. She currently lives in Portland, Oregon, USA.

WHY WE LOVE KALE

KALE HAS GONE FROM HIPPIE WHOLEFOOD TO QUEEN OF GREENS, KING OF CABBAGES AND ALL-ROUND VEGETABLE STAR. RIGHTLY SO, CONSIDERING EVERYTHING THE CRUCIFEROUS VEGETABLE HAS GOING FOR IT!

KALE IS GOOD FOR YOU

Kale, once just a leafy green adored by vegans and vegetarians, has gone mainstream and not without reason. This vegetable tops the charts when it comes to what you need for a healthy diet – and it tastes delicious too.

* **IRON:** One of the main benefits of kale and a reason why kale is always on the plate of those that do not eat meat is because it is chock-full of iron. In fact, per calorie, kale contains more iron than beef.

* **CALCIUM:** Kale is one of many leafy greens that are very high in calcium. Some studies have proven that the calcium obtained from greens is better for you than the calcium you would intake from milk and dairy products. In fact, there is more calcium generally per serving of kale than milk and the body absorbs it better.

* **FIBRE:** On the Aggregate Nutrient Density Index, kale scores a 1,000 at the top of the ratings. Most people do not eat the daily recommendation of 25 g (¾ oz.) of fibre for women and 38 g (1⅓ oz.) for men, but adding kale into your meals is an easy way to meet this goal.

* **VITAMINS AND ANTIOXIDANTS:** Kale contains high amounts of vitamins C, A and K (see Need to Know, page 12) to assist with vision and bone health and to help strengthen the immune system.

* **ALKALINE:** Kale is considered an alkaline vegetable, and with many modern diets including far too many acidic foods, kale helps to balance things out. In macrobiotic theory, where the diet aims to maintain the yin and yang within the body, kale is a key leafy green when it comes to balancing the yang and further aiding in detoxification of the blood.

KALE IS A VERSATILE VEGETABLE

There are countless ways to cook and enjoy kale. What other vegetable can make a salad, smoothie, juice, crisp, cookie and a sautéed side dish? Kale can! It's not very often that a simple leafy green can be used in so many fun and interesting ways. While you may have tried kale for the first time because of its popularity, you will continue to eat kale because you can use it in a morning smoothie or add it to a pasta dish at the last minute.

KALE IS EASY TO COOK

There are so many wonderful recipes to try using kale, but here are two basic ways to prepare kale for a night when you just want something simple, green and healthy.

* STEAM: Do not boil, but lightly steam. In a small saucepan, boil around 2 cm (¾ in.) of water, then place a vegetable steamer or heat-proof colander containing the kale on top of the pan. Steam until the kale is bright green and then drain. Add olive oil and salt, lemon juice or gamasio (sesame salt) for flavour.

* SAUTÉ: In a medium saucepan, heat olive oil and garlic and add chopped kale. Chilli flakes will add a little spicy heat. Continue to stir until the greens are cooked, about 7 minutes. If needed, add a tablespoon of water after about 3 minutes to add some additional moisture.

KALE IS EASY TO GROW

If you have access to a small garden or even a balcony with a few planters, growing kale is really simple. All you need to do is plant a few seeds and you will be able to harvest your own kale almost year-round (although this does vary depending on where you live). For more information on the ideal situation for growth of different kale varieties, see pages 16–17.

It is recommended that you germinate seeds first in a seed tray and then plant them when the seedlings are 10–12 cm (4–4½ in.) high. Place the plants about 50 cm (20 in.) apart and in rows 50–60 cm (20–24 in.) apart. The plants should receive plenty of sunlight and be watered daily.

If you are planting kale on a balcony, place seeds around 2–3 cm (¾–1¼ in.) below the soil, cover and water daily. Sprouts will appear within a week.

THE KALE MASSAGE

You might think it sounds crazy to actually massage a vegetable, but this is a key step for any kale salad. When the kale is chopped and in the salad bowl, and before toppings are added, add the dressing of choice and massage the kale with your hands – with love of course. Kneading for 1-2 minutes marinates and softens the leaves. Let the salad sit for 30–60 minutes before eating.

NEED TO KNOW: For those with existing thyroid issues, please consult a doctor before consuming kale or cruciferous vegetables. The high amounts of vitamin K may conflict with certain thyroid medications.

10 WAYS TO EAT MORE KALE

1 HOMEBAKED

Finely chop a handful or two of de-stemmed kale and throw it into cake, bread or muffin batter to add extra fibre. Most people won't even notice the added green but the health benefits are definitely there. Try the Triple Rich Hidden Gem Brownies on page 167.

2 MORNINGS

Kale belongs at breakfast. What better way to start the day? Add kale to your scrambled eggs, as with the Scrambled Tofu on page 38. For a sweeter start, try adding kale to homemade granola like the Crunchy Kale Granola on page 32.

3 PARTY STARTERS

Add kale to dips like Baked Kale and Artichoke Dip on page 57 or share a plate of Ginger Shiitake Avocado Summer Rolls at your next get together (page 58). Kale crisps make a great treat for parties and kids will love the Pesto Alfredo Kale Crisps on page 52.

4 ANCIENT GRAINS

There are so many ancient grains to try and what better way than with kale? Quinoa, farro, brown rice, millet and more make great side dishes or a filling lunch. Try the Kale, Parmesan and Lemon Pearl Barley Risotto on page 109.

5 SMOOTHIES

Creamy smoothies are good for any time of day and they are even better with a bunch of kale. Start with the Tropical Sunshine Smoothie on page 22.

7 SOUPS

This is one of the easiest ways to include more kale. Wash, chop and throw a few handfuls of kale into any hearty soup, or for something new try the Spicy Chicken and Kale Kimchi Soup on page 123.

6 SALADS

Do you have a few kale virgins coming over for dinner? Make a regular salad and add in a handful of de-stemmed, finely chopped kale to add a hearty flavour. Or test out the Vietnamese Chicken Salad on page 141; the dressing will make anyone love the leafy green.

8 PIZZAS

Charred kale can turn pizza from the 'easy' dinner into the 'easy and healthy' dinner. The vibrant greens look beautiful simply set on a crisp, golden base in the Pizza with Kale and Taleggio recipe on page 92.

9 HAPPY HOUR

You wouldn't expect to include kale with a cocktail, but the earthy, fresh taste pairs well with spirits, too. Cool down on a summer day with the Kale and Cucumber Margarita on page 80 or the Dirty Kale Martini on page 85.

10 SWEET TOOTH

You don't need to feel guilty about satisfying a sweet craving when you add some kale. Enjoy something sweet with extra vitamins and antioxidants as well, like the Zesty Power Bites on page 164 or Sweet Green Pancakes on page 35.

TYPES OF KALE

Kale is part of the brassica family, with the Latin name *Brassica oleracea* Acephala. The brassica family consists of all cabbages like broccoli, cauliflower, turnips, Brussels sprouts, radishes and more. Kale is thought to have evolved from wild cabbage plants and mentions were recorded thousands of years ago in Asia Minor and throughout the Mediterranean. As plants were continually bred, eventually headed cabbages became more popular to grow and consume (they also last longer after harvesting). In many countries and cultures, kale is only grown for animal consumption and it is not until recently, due to the vegetable's immense health benefits, that kale has come into its own as a superfood and once again has a prominent place on plates.

Traditionally, like all cabbages, kale is a cold-weather vegetable. The general season for harvest is September to February or March. In some cultures, kale will not be harvested until after the first frost, as the vegetable withstands colder temperatures and some say the taste is sweeter after a frost.

Kale seasonality varies on location but the ideal situation for optimum growth is:
* Fertile, well-drained soil, high in organic matter
* Soil pH around 6.0–7.5
* Consistent moisture will produce best quality and highest yields
* Ideal temperature for growth is 7–8°C/44–46°F (low) and 20–25°C/68–77°F (high)
* Growth is possible in warmer weather but the plant will grow faster and age more quickly.
There are three varieties of kale that are very common in supermarkets and farmers' markets. Within these there are different seed varietals.

CURLY GREEN
The name says it all! Curly green kale is the most common variety grown and sold. As the name suggests, the leaves are large and dark green with curly edges. An earthy but mild taste, this is most often the variety of kale that people try first.

CAVOLO NERO
This variety has many names including Tuscan kale, black kale, dinosaur kale and lacinato. Many refer to it as cavolo nero. The leaves are longer and thinner and less curly than curly green, with leaves that are blistered and said to resemble the skin of a dinosaur (hence the name). The taste is slightly stronger than curly green kale but still is fantastic in all kale recipes.

RED RUSSIAN
The leaves of red Russian kale are slightly thicker and tougher than curly green or cavolo nero kale leaves but share their earthy taste. The leaves can range from hues of reds to blueish-greens to greenish-purples and vary depending on seed variety. This type of kale is great in soups and sautés.

REDBOR
Redbor kale is less likely to be found in supermarkets or farmers' markets, but the vibrant purple colour of the leaves is stunning and always stands out among the rest. The leaves are also curly and their taste is mild and similar to that of curly green kale.

ORNAMENTAL

In some countries – France for example – kale is grown for ornamental purposes in gardens and parks. Be aware that this kale should not be consumed just in case the plants have been heavily sprayed with pesticides.

BABY KALE

All of these varieties (except ornamental) can be picked when the leaves are smaller, which many people refer to as baby kale. Baby kale is more tender and, as a result, it's perfect for salads or salad mixes, or for any raw kale recipe that might benefit from less time spent on the kale massage.

BRUSSELKALE

There are a few names for this new vegetable hybrid (non-GMO) of kale and Brussels sprouts, which grows with a small Brussels sprouts bud and tiny kale leaves. Among them are Kalettes™, Flower Sprouts, or BrusselKale. Bred by a British seed company, Tozer Seeds, it is not until recently that this new variety has been marketed and is now available in the United States.

COOKING WITH KALE

The beauty of kale is that it is so versatile. For the photography in this book we used curly kale, but any kind can be used for the recipes (unless otherwise specified). Why not mix it up and use a few different varieties or try each one and find your favourite?

HOW TO PREPARE KALE

CHOOSING KALE

When shopping for kale, there are a few things to look out for. Kale should be bought as fresh as possible so that it lasts longer in your fridge. Avoid bagged kale if you can, as it is most likely older and not as good quality. As you will see, prepping fresh whole kale leaves is easy and does not take a lot of time. Try to purchase organic kale if it is available – kale can attract pests in the fields, and conventional farmers will spray the plants heavily to keep insects away.

PREPARING KALE

If you can wash and dry the kale the same day that you buy it, it will last longer.

* **WASHING KALE**: To wash kale, run each leaf underneath cold water and use your hands to remove any dirt or other remains from the fields (if it's organic you might find a caterpillar or two). Do this on both the front and back, moving up and down the stem as well as to each side of the leaf. Be extra diligent with the curly varieties. If you want to de-stem kale (see how to, right), this is a great time to do it.

* **DRYING**: An easy way to dry kale is using a salad spinner. Place washed kale inside and spin for 2–3 cycles. If you do not have a salad spinner, you can pat the leaves dry with kitchen towel. If you plan on eating a lot more kale in the future, a salad spinner is a wise investment. If you are making kale crisps and don't have a spinner, people have been known to use a hair-dryer to dry their kale!

DE-STEMMING

Many recipes will call for kale to be 'de-stemmed'. This is the simple process of removing the leafy part of kale from the thick and tough stem. Hold the kale leaf in one hand. Fold the two kale leaf sides together and rip from the bottom of the stem to the top.

Recipes usually suggest this because the stem is too tough or fibrous for the dish. For example, raw kale salads and smoothies are better with de-stemmed kale, so the vegetable is easier to consume. You can save stems for juicing or for making homemade vegetable stock.

CUTTING AND CHOPPING

There are a few ways to cut and chop kale but it depends on what the recipe calls for and also how you are serving it.

* **CHIFFONADE**: For those new to kale and specifically new to raw kale salads, the tougher texture of the leaves might seem like hard work, so finely chopping kale with a chiffonade method will make the kale easier to experience for the first time. As time goes on, kale salads don't always have to require fine chopping and kale can be chopped quickly in larger pieces.

* **BITE-SIZE**: For smoothies, sautés, soups, pastas and more, kale does not need to be chopped in a uniform fashion and can quickly be cut into bite-size pieces using a normal vegetable knife.

* **STRIPS**: For some dishes, you might want to cut the kale into more uniform strips. This can be done with kale that is not de-stemmed. Fold the kale so it makes a half-leaf shape and cut into

horizontal strips. For this method and all kale that is not already de-stemmed, it is advised only to cut the stem that is attached to part of the leaf and to discard the bottom part of the stem.

STORING KALE

When the kale is dry, store in a sealable plastic bag. A plastic bag with a twist-tie will work just fine. Remove all the air and the kale will keep for up to 10 days in the fridge. It is important that the majority of moisture is gone to ensure that the kale does not partially freeze.

* FREEZING: Freezing kale is a great idea if you want to purchase locally grown kale in bulk and enjoy it at a later time or to have on-hand for a quick weeknight dinner. You can freeze kale using two different methods.

* RAW: Wash, dry and chop to your preferred size. Kale does not need to be de-stemmed but you will not be able to de-stem it after it is frozen. Kale does not need to be as dry as it does if drying for immediate use. Store in freezer-safe plastic bags.

* PRECOOKED: Wash the kale and de-stem, if preferred. Quickly blanch kale in a pot of boiling water for 30 seconds. Using tongs or a wide slotted spoon, remove and place the kale in a bowl of iced water to cool it down quickly. Dry the kale with kitchen towel. Place into freezer-safe plastic bags.

Another option for precooked frozen kale is to initially freeze it in ice cube trays. This makes small, individual frozen portions for daily use in smoothies. Place precooked kale into ice cube trays and freeze overnight. Remove each kale cube and place into a freezer-safe bag.

Kale lasts for around 6 months in the freezer, and although it will not work for recipes that call for fresh, raw kale, it's a great option for many other kale dishes.

NOTES ON OTHER INGREDIENTS

EGGS: The recipes throughout this book use medium, free-range eggs. Medium eggs typically weigh 57 g (2 oz.), the equivalent of 3¼ tablespoons. Eggs that are free-range mean the hens that laid them are uncaged and have some access to outdoor space, hopefully allowing them to engage in natural behaviours.

BUTTER: When you recreate these recipes, the butter used should be unsalted unless otherwise stated in the recipe. This allows you to control the salt level in your cooking and customize it to your taste by adding as much or little salt as you like. Salted butter can also mask other flavours, therefore downplaying the taste of the rest of your ingredients.

SALT: All recipes in the book use table salt unless noted. The grains of table salt are finer and more uniform than other types of salt and this allows them to be more evenly distributed.

SUGAR: Unless otherwise specified, granulated white sugar is the sugar used in all recipes. Granulated sugar gives the best baking results, as the larger crystals allow more air into the mixture, therefore creating a lighter texture when baked.

FRUITS AND VEGETABLES: For fruits and vegetables that vary in size (e.g. potatoes, onions, carrots), please assume that they are medium unless otherwise stated in the recipe.

BREAKFAST & BRUNCH

TROPICAL SUNSHINE SMOOTHIE

REFRESHING GREEN JUICE

KALE AND MIXED BERRY SMOOTHIE BOWL

CRUNCHY KALE GRANOLA

SWEET GREEN PANCAKES

BAKED EGGS, KALE AND GRUYÈRE

KALE AND MUSHROOM BREAKFAST MUFFINS

KALE AND RED PEPPER POTATO CAKES

KALE SHAKSHUKA

CREAMY KALE GALETTE

Recipe on page 45

TROPICAL SUNSHINE SMOOTHIE

(VG)

SERVES	2
PREP	5 minutes

YOU WILL NEED

225 ml (7½ fl oz.) cold coconut water

225 ml (7½ fl oz.) cold coconut milk (or your favourite milk)

140 g (5 oz.) kale, washed and de-stemmed

3 large dried Medjool dates, pitted

1 fresh or frozen ripe banana

handful of ice cubes (if using fresh fruit)

165 g (5¾ oz.) fresh or frozen pineapple pieces

½ teaspoon ground cinnamon

flaked coconut, for garnish

FREE FROM
DAIRY, GLUTEN & WHEAT

STARTING THE DAY WITH A SMOOTHIE IS QUICK, EASY AND NUTRITIOUS, SO IT'S GOOD TO HAVE A FEW RECIPES UP YOUR SLEEVE. THIS IS A FAVOURITE THAT YOU CAN TURN TO AGAIN AND AGAIN.

1 Combine the coconut water, coconut milk, kale and dates in a food processor or high power liquidizer. Blend at the highest speed until the mixture is completely smooth.

2 Add the banana, ice (if using), pineapple and cinnamon and continue to blend until smooth. Pour into glasses and top with flaked coconut.

RISE AND SHINE: These smoothies are great first thing in the morning or any time of day as a workout recovery.

TROPICAL SUNSHINE SMOOTHIE VARIATIONS

ADDING A FEW DIFFERENT FLAVOURS TO YOUR SMOOTHIE CAN TRANSFORM YOUR MORNING. TRANSPORT YOURSELF TO SUMMERTIME WITH JUICY PEACHES, WHIP UP AN ISLAND HOLIDAY IN A GLASS WITH TROPICAL FRUITS, OR CREATE A RICH AND DECADENT CHOCOLATE TREAT — WHILE STILL PROVIDING YOUR BODY WITH HEALTHY NUTRIENTS.

VG DF GF WF

PEACHY CREAM SMOOTHIE

Start with the basic smoothie base of coconut water, coconut milk, fresh kale, dates, fresh or frozen banana and ice. In place of the pineapple and cinnamon, add 2 fresh pitted peaches, half an avocado and 40 g (1½ oz.) dried apricots, and blend until smooth.

VG DF GF WF

LIME AND COCONUT KALE SMOOTHIE

Add 25 g (¾ oz.) grated fresh coconut and the juice and grated zest of 2 large limes (reserving a small amount of zest for garnish) to the basic smoothie base of cold coconut water, cold coconut milk, fresh kale, dates, fresh or frozen banana and ice. Omit the pineapple and cinnamon and blend until smooth. Top with flaked coconut and lime zest for serving.

VG DF GF WF

DREAMY DOUBLE CHOCOLATE SMOOTHIE

Begin with the basic smoothie base of cold coconut water, cold coconut milk, fresh kale, dates, fresh or frozen banana and ice. Substitute the pineapple, cinnamon and coconut garnish with 40 g (1½ oz.) vegan dark chocolate chips, 30 g (1 oz.) cocoa powder (or chocolate protein powder), 1 tablespoon pure vanilla extract and a pinch of sea salt, and blend until smooth.

COCONUT

Coconut is a true superfood, rich in good fats that have a positive effect on our health in many ways. Increased energy and better brain function are among the benefits of coconut, which is a medium chain triglyceride helping to burn body fat and cholesterol. Versatility is also a benefit – coconut oil can be used in smoothies, sautés and baking. Out of the kitchen, the oil is a great moisturizer for your skin or hair.

REFRESHING GREEN JUICE

SERVES	4
PREP	15 minutes

YOU WILL NEED

2 carrots

1 large cucumber

450 g (1 lb.) kale, washed

2 garlic cloves

2 lemons, peel and pith removed

6 celery stalks

bunch of fresh flat-leaf parsley

bunch of fresh coriander

fine sea salt, to taste

FREE FROM
DAIRY, GLUTEN
& WHEAT

MELLOW CUCUMBER AND CELERY BRING OUT THE BEST IN THE KALE, WHILE LEMON AND HERBS ADD JUST THE RIGHT AMOUNT OF BRIGHTNESS AND COMPLEXITY.

1 Feed the ingredients into a juicer in the order listed. This will maximize the yield. Stir the juices together until they are well combined.

2 Divide between four glasses and serve immediately.

GREEN JUICE VARIATIONS

ASIAN GREEN JUICE Swap the lemons for limes and add a small knob of fresh ginger root. Instead of salt, finish with a few dashes of tamari or gluten-free soya sauce.

SPICY GREEN JUICE A few dashes of your favourite hot sauce will complement this juice beautifully, or add a couple of tomatoes to the juicer for a gazpacho-inspired drink.

GREEN SMOOTHIE For a more substantial drink, turn this juice into a smoothie by adding avocado. In both savoury and sweet green smoothies, avocados can add heft and creaminess. Their mild flavour plays well with a wide variety of other ingredients, and their effect on texture is unparalleled. Just whirl 250 ml (8½ fl oz.) juice in the liquidizer with half a pitted avocado and serve.

KALE AND MIXED BERRY SMOOTHIE BOWL (VG)

SERVES	4
PREP	15 minutes

YOU WILL NEED

200 g (7 oz.) kale, washed and de-stemmed

150 g (5¼ oz.) blueberries

150 g (5¼ oz.) raspberries

100 g (3½ oz.) almonds

300 ml (½ pint) almond milk

2–3 tablespoons honey, to taste

4 ice cubes

FOR THE CRUNCHY TOPPING

50 g (1¾ oz.) walnuts

50 g (1¾ oz.) slivered almonds

50 g (1¾ oz.) grated fresh coconut

25 g (¾ oz.) sunflower seeds

25 g (¾ oz.) chia seeds

FREE FROM
DAIRY, GLUTEN & WHEAT

ADD FRESH KALE TO MIXED BERRIES, BLITZ TO MAKE A THICK SMOOTHIE, AND SERVE IN A BOWL WITH A CRUNCHY SEED AND NUT TOPPING FOR A POWER-PACKED BREAKFAST OR SNACK.

1 You will need a powerful liquidizer or food processor for this recipe. Place all the smoothie ingredients in the liquidizer and blend until smooth; adjust the thickness to taste by adding more ice cubes. (If your liquidizer jug is on the small side, you may need to make this in two batches.)

2 Place all the topping ingredients in a food processor (cleaned from making the smoothie if required), and pulse until just chopped and still crunchy.

3 For serving, pour the smoothie into individual bowls and sprinkle the crunchy topping over the smoothie.

DELICIOUS AND NUTRITIOUS: The greens add texture and fibre as well as counting towards your five-a-day.

SMOOTHIE BOWL VARIATIONS
THESE FABULOUS ALTERNATIVE SMOOTHIE BOWL RECIPE IDEAS WILL CERTAINLY PERK YOU UP, WITH ADDED FRUIT, NUTS, SEEDS AND GRAINS THAT ARE PERFECT FOR YOUR DAILY HEALTH REQUIREMENTS.

V **GF** **WF**

TROPICAL DETOX SMOOTHIE BOWL
Make this detox smoothie bowl for after the party is over! Packed with probiotic yoghurt for health, the coconut topping adds an extra tropical taste. Blend 200 g (7 oz.) chopped kale with 1 small fresh diced pineapple to aid digestion, 600 ml (21 fl oz.) probiotic natural yoghurt, 25 g (¾ oz.) fresh ginger root, 1 cored apple, 2 tablespoons honey and a handful of ice cubes. Blend until smooth and pour into bowls before sprinkling with 150 g (5¼ oz.) toasted grated fresh coconut. You can use probiotic fruit yoghurts, too, for an extra fruity flavour – just omit the honey.

V **GF** **WF**

CARROT CAKE SMOOTHIE BOWL
Get that carrot cake taste in a smoothie bowl without a trace of fat or flour! Blend the following ingredients until smooth: 100 g (3½ oz.) chopped kale, 4 large chopped carrots, 4 large frozen bananas, 600 ml (21 fl oz.) milk, 2 teaspoons ground cinnamon and a handful of ice cubes. Pour into bowls and top with 100 g (3½ oz.) chopped, toasted walnuts mixed with 2 tablespoons desiccated coconut. Use almond, soya or coconut milk for a dairy-free version.

VG **DF** **GF** **WF**

GREEN GODDESS SMOOTHIE BOWL
Kale, grapes, apples and kiwifruits make up this vibrant green smoothie, and a combination of three super seeds adds a fabulous, healthy crunch. Place 100 g (3½ oz.) chopped kale, 100 g (3½ oz.) seedless green grapes, 2 cored green apples and 4 chopped kiwifruits into a liquidizer. Add 300 ml (½ pint) almond milk and a handful of ice cubes and blitz until smooth. Serve in bowls with a mixture of 50 g (1¾ oz.) toasted sesame seeds, 25 g (¾ oz.) toasted chia seeds and 25 g (¾ oz.) toasted pumpkin seeds scattered on top.

NUTS

Nuts not only taste delicious, but they are an essential ingredient in lots of baking recipes, as well as being fabulous when added to salads and savoury dishes. High in dietary fibre and minerals such as potassium and magnesium, they are also rich in bone-building calcium and protein. Scatter them over desserts, pancakes, porridge and salads for an extra healthy boost, or add them to sweet bakes, tarts and cakes for an afternoon treat. Nuts are also a nice treat when roasted in honey and served as a snack with cocktails.

CRUNCHY KALE GRANOLA

(V)

MAKES	1 large glass jar
PREP	5 minutes
COOK	35–45 minutes

YOU WILL NEED

300 g (10½ oz.) dried oats

200 g (7 oz.) kale, washed, de-stemmed and finely chopped

30 g (1 oz.) walnuts

20 g (¾ oz.) grated fresh coconut

120 ml (4 fl oz.) olive oil

60 ml (2 fl oz.) maple syrup

30 g (1 oz.) dried fruit (raisins or cherries are good options)

FREE FROM
DAIRY & WHEAT

GRANOLA IS A MUST-HAVE STAPLE FOR ANY PANTRY AND FOR ANY BREAKFAST PAIRING. THE ADDED KALE IN THIS RECIPE BRINGS SOME GREEN GOODNESS TO YOUR MORNING.

1 Preheat the oven to 100°C/200°F/Gas Mark ½. Line a baking tray with aluminium foil.

2 Mix the oats, kale, walnuts and coconut in a bowl. Add the olive oil and mix, trying to coat as much of the mixture as possible. Add the maple syrup and mix, again coating as much of the mixture as possible.

3 Pour and spread the mixture evenly on the baking tray. Bake for 35–45 minutes (ovens differ so it's best to monitor and mix throughout the baking time to avoid burning).

4 Allow to cool, then mix in the dried fruit. Store in an airtight jar for up to 3 weeks.

SWEET GREEN PANCAKES

(V)

MAKES	18–20 pancakes
PREP	5 minutes
COOK	10 minutes

YOU WILL NEED

3 tablespoons flaxseed, freshly ground

80 ml (2¾ fl oz.) warm water

75 g (2½ oz) kale

240 ml (8 fl oz.) sweetened vanilla almond milk

130 g (4½ oz.) gluten-free plain flour

50 g (1¾ oz.) sugar

1 tablespoon baking powder

your favourite pancake topping, for serving

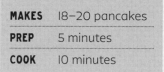

FREE FROM
DAIRY, GLUTEN
& WHEAT

THIS RECIPE MAKES VIBRANT GREEN PANCAKES THAT ARE JUST THE RIGHT AMOUNT OF SWEET, WITH A VERY SLIGHT 'GREEN' FLAVOUR THAT IS A REMINDER YOU ARE GETTING YOUR VITAMINS IN.

1 Combine the ground flaxseeds with the water and set aside for 15 minutes to form a gel (this is the equivalent of 3 eggs).

2 Meanwhile, scrub the kale leaves clean under running water with your hands, squeezing and wringing it out as you go. Remove the stems.

3 Put the kale, flax gel and milk in a food processor or liquidizer and blend to a liquid.

4 Combine the flour, sugar and baking powder in a bowl. Pour the kale mixture into the dry ingredients and whisk to a smooth batter.

5 Use a 60 ml (2 fl oz.) measure to pour the batter onto a heated griddle pan set over a low heat (cooking over a low heat keeps the bright green colour), flipping once when cooked through and golden brown. Keep the pancakes warm as you make the remaining pancakes.

SERVING SUGGESTION: These pancakes are great simply served with your favourite nut butter, dairy butter or vegan spread.

BAKED EGGS, KALE AND GRUYÈRE

(v)

SERVES	I
PREP	15 minutes
COOK	15–25 minutes

YOU WILL NEED

2 tablespoons olive oil

50 g (1¾ oz.) kale, washed, de-stemmed and roughly chopped

chilli flakes (optional)

2 eggs

50 g (1¾ oz.) grated Gruyère or Comté cheese (anything sharp will do)

salt and freshly ground black pepper

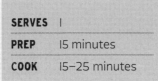

FREE FROM
GLUTEN & WHEAT

MANY PEOPLE WOULDN'T THINK THAT KALE IS THE PERFECT ADDITION TO BREAKFAST, BUT IT PAIRS BRILLIANTLY WITH FAVOURITES LIKE EGGS AND SCRAMBLED TOFU.

1 Preheat the oven to 180°C/350°F/Gas Mark 4.

2 Heat the olive oil in a frying pan over a medium heat for I minute. Add the chopped kale to the frying pan and sauté for 4–5 minutes, stirring occasionally. Add a sprinkle of salt, freshly ground black pepper and chilli flakes, if using.

3 When the kale is sautéed, add it to an individual ovenproof dish. Crack the eggs on top of the kale and sprinkle with the grated cheese.

4 Bake for 20 minutes for a soft yolk or 25 minutes for a hard yolk and serve sprinkled with more chilli flakes, if desired.

BAKED EGG VARIATIONS

IF YOU DON'T HAVE QUITE ENOUGH TIME TO BAKE YOUR EGGS, SCRAMBLED EGGS MAKE A QUICK MORNING MEAL PACKED WITH PROTEIN. YOU CAN CREATE AN EQUALLY PROTEIN-PACKED VEGAN BREAKFAST WITH SCRAMBLED TOFU.

V GF WF

SCRAMBLED EGGS AND KALE

For a simpler and faster breakfast, instead of baking the eggs in the oven, whisk 8 eggs in a small bowl and then add to the sautéed kale. Mix together until the eggs are cooked and scrambled. Serve with freshly ground black pepper and cheese if you like. Serves 4.

V GF WF

TEXAS SCRAMBLE

This is the same as simple scrambled eggs and kale, but a few extra ingredients give it a Texan twist. Heat 2 tablespoons olive oil in a saucepan over a medium heat for 1 minute. Add 3–4 washed and diced spring onions and stir for 2 minutes until translucent. Add 1 seeded and cubed pepper and half a finely diced jalapeño pepper (if desired), and continue to stir for another 3–4 minutes until cooked. Add 400 g (14 oz.) washed, de-stemmed and chopped kale to the saucepan and sauté for another 4–5 minutes. Stir in a sprinkle of salt and freshly ground black pepper. Add 1 tin (400 g/14 oz.) drained and rinsed black beans and continue to stir. Add 1 teaspoon ground cumin for extra flavour. While the ingredients are cooking, whisk 8 eggs and 50 g (1¾ oz.) grated cheddar cheese in a large bowl. Add them to the saucepan and mix until the eggs are scrambled. Serve with freshly chopped coriander. Serves 4.

VG DF GF WF

SCRAMBLED TOFU

Try making your scramble with tofu for a vegan alternative. Crumble 1 packet (500 g/1 lb. 2 oz.) drained tofu into a medium-size bowl with your hands. Add 20 g (¾ oz.) nutritional yeast, 1 tablespoon curry powder and 2 tablespoons tamari or soya sauce and mix together. Heat 2 tablespoons olive oil in a saucepan over a medium heat. Add 1 diced spring onion and stir for 2–3 minutes until translucent. Add 400 g (14 oz.) washed, de-stemmed and chopped kale and sauté for 4–5 minutes. Add the tofu mixture and cook for another 10 minutes. Serve with a dash of salt and freshly ground black pepper if desired. Serves 2–3.

EGGS

Eggs are essential in a vegetarian cook's kitchen and are a 'complete protein' ingredient; they boast a host of vitamins such as B1, B2, B3, B5, B6, B12 and choline. Rich in folic acid too, they are nature's perfect packet of goodness. Scramble them, poach them, fry them or coddle them – they are one of the handiest ingredients for an easy, protein-packed breakfast, as well as being necessary in cake and baking recipes.

KALE AND MUSHROOM BREAKFAST MUFFINS

(V)

MAKES	12
PREP	15 minutes
COOK	20 minutes

YOU WILL NEED

spray oil, for greasing

2 tablespoons olive oil

1 onion, diced

200 g (7 oz.) fresh mushrooms, wiped, trimmed and sliced

200 g (7 oz.) kale, chopped

4 eggs, beaten with 4 tablespoons milk

50 g (1¾ oz.) grated vegetarian Parmesan cheese, plus a little extra for sprinkling

2 tablespoons fresh basil, roughly chopped

salt and freshly ground black pepper

chutney, for serving

FREE FROM GLUTEN & WHEAT

THESE GLUTEN-FREE MUFFINS ARE PACKED WITH VEGETABLES AND FLAVOUR; EAT THEM WARM FOR BREAKFAST OR BRUNCH, OR ALLOW THEM TO COOL FOR A SNACK ON THE GO.

1 Preheat the oven to 200°C/400°F/Gas Mark 6 and coat a 12-cup muffin tin with the spray oil.

2 Heat the olive oil in a large frying pan and add the onions. Fry for 5 minutes before adding the mushrooms; fry for 3–4 minutes, until softened, then add the kale and cook for a further 5 minutes.

3 Put the cooked vegetables in a large bowl and season to taste with salt and freshly ground black pepper. Add the eggs, cheese and basil, and mix to make a batter.

4 Spoon the batter into the prepared muffin tin, sprinkle a little extra Parmesan over the top, and bake for 20 minutes, until well risen, golden brown and puffy.

5 Leave to cool slightly in the tin before easing the muffins out and letting them cool completely on a wire cooling rack.

6 Serve warm with chutney or grilled tomatoes for breakfast or cold with salad for a light lunch or snack.

KALE AND RED PEPPER POTATO CAKES

(V)

SERVES	4
PREP	40 minutes
COOK	15 minutes

YOU WILL NEED

750 g (1 lb. 10 oz.) potatoes, peeled and diced

1 red pepper, seeded and finely diced

150 g (5¼ oz.) kale, shredded

spray oil

1 egg, beaten

4 tablespoons cottage cheese

2 tablespoons plain flour, for coating

salt and freshly ground black pepper

soured cream and smoked paprika, for serving

DELICIOUS LITTLE KALE POTATO CAKES WITH RED PEPPER AND COTTAGE CHEESE, THESE PATTIES ARE LOW FAT BUT HIGH IN PROTEIN, MAKING THEM THE IDEAL BREAKFAST DISH TO KEEP YOU GOING UNTIL LUNCHTIME.

1 Boil the potatoes in a saucepan of water until soft and then drain and mash until smooth.

2 Fry the peppers and kale in a large wok that has been coated with spray oil. Fry until the peppers are soft and the kale has wilted.

3 Add the peppers and kale to the mashed potatoes and mix well. Season to taste with salt and pepper, add the beaten egg and cottage cheese and mix well. Put the mixture in the fridge to chill for 30 minutes (or overnight).

4 When you are ready to cook the potato cakes, heat a large frying pan and coat with oil. Shape the mixture into balls, flatten them slightly and then dust with flour.

5 Fry over a gentle heat for 3–4 minutes each side, until golden brown and crispy. Serve immediately with a dollop of soured cream and a dusting of smoked paprika. For a hearty, non-vegetarian breakfast, serve with fried eggs and griddled bacon.

KALE AND PEPPER POTATO CAKE VARIATIONS

THREE MORE IDEAS FOR THESE TASTY KALE POTATO CAKES, WITH ADDED INGREDIENTS AND DIFFERENT SERVING SUGGESTIONS TO SUIT ALL THE FAMILY'S LIKES AND DISLIKES AS WELL AS SPECIAL DIETARY REQUIREMENTS.

HAM, CHEESE AND KALE POTATO CAKES

For those who want a higher protein potato cake, these provide the perfect breakfast dish. In place of the pepper, add 100 g (3½ oz.) chopped cooked ham and replace the cottage cheese with 100 g (3½ oz.) grated mature cheddar cheese. Make the cakes as before, adding the chopped ham and cheese to the mashed potatoes, beaten egg and cooked kale. Season to taste with salt and freshly ground black pepper. Serve with homemade tomato ketchup and fried mushrooms.

BUBBLE AND SQUEAK POTATO CAKES

These potato cakes make great use of any leftover vegetables from yesterday's lunch or dinner. Finely dice any cooked vegetables you may have on hand, such as cabbage, carrots, sprouts, chard, broccoli and peas. Mash any potatoes you have left over – if there aren't enough potatoes left, boil some more to make about 600 g (I lb. 5 oz.) mash. Add all the diced leftover vegetables, including 50–75 g (1¾–2½ oz.) cooked kale, to the potatoes, plus I beaten egg and lots of freshly ground black pepper. Shape and fry as before. Serve with a poached egg, fried tomatoes and mushrooms for a complete vegetarian breakfast or brunch.

MUSHROOMS ON KALE AND POTATO CAKES

Put a tasty spin on traditional mushrooms on toast and serve garlic-fried mushrooms on crispy kale potato cakes for a lazy weekend brunch. Make the kale and potato cakes following the main recipe, but serve them with 250 g (9 oz.) sliced mushrooms that have been fried in 4 tablespoons (50 g/1¾ oz.) butter with 4 diced garlic cloves. Spoon the garlic mushrooms over the cooked potato cakes and garnish with a lemon wedge and freshly chopped parsley. You can also serve this with grilled bacon or sausages for a non-vegetarian version.

KALE SHAKSHUKA

(V)

SERVES	3
PREP	10 minutes
COOK	35–45 minutes

YOU WILL NEED

60 ml (2 fl oz.) olive oil

1 onion, diced

1 red pepper, seeded and diced

1 teaspoon fine sea salt

6 garlic cloves, minced

1 teaspoon ground cumin

1½ teaspoons ground sweet Hungarian paprika

¼ teaspoon chilli flakes

1 tin (790 g/28 oz.) chopped tomatoes

12 leaves cavolo nero, washed, de-stemmed and finely chopped

6 eggs

freshly ground black pepper

toast, for serving

(pictured on page 21)

FREE FROM GLUTEN & WHEAT

SHAKSHUKA LOOKS LIKE IMPRESSIVE BRUNCH FARE, BUT IT HAS A SECRET: IT'S REALLY SOME OF THE WORLD'S FINEST COMFORT FOOD, OF NORTH AFRICAN ORIGIN. THIS INTERPRETATION IS SIMPLE, FAIRLY QUICK TO MAKE AND NOT OVERLY SPICY.

1 Heat the olive oil in a large, heavy frying pan over a medium-high heat. Add the onion, pepper and a sprinkle of the salt and cook for 5–10 minutes, stirring from time to time, until softened.

2 Add the garlic, cumin, paprika and chilli flakes and cook for a further 2 minutes, stirring the mixture frequently, until the spices are toasted and fragrant.

3 Add the tomatoes, kale, remaining salt and a few good grinds of black pepper and stir together. Simmer for 15 minutes, until the sauce is slightly thickened and the kale is tender. Remove from the heat.

4 Create a small divot in the sauce for each egg, and then crack the eggs into the pan. Cover and simmer for about 10 minutes, until the egg whites are set and yolks still runny (or until the eggs reach your desired consistency). Serve with toast.

CUSTOMIZE YOUR SHAKSHUKA

■ Add more heat as desired by increasing the chilli flakes or adding a minced chilli when you sauté the onion and pepper.

■ You can also add feta cheese to this dish for added creamy texture and taste. Just dot 115 g (4 oz.) of crumbled feta into the sauce before adding the eggs. Sprinkle with freshly chopped flat-leaf parsley before serving.

■ To stretch this dish for a larger crowd, use an extra-large frying pan and drop in a couple of additional eggs.

CREAMY KALE GALETTE

(V)

SERVES	I
PREP	I5 minutes
COOK	20 minutes

YOU WILL NEED

1 tablespoon olive oil

50 g (1¾ oz.) kale, washed, de-stemmed and finely chopped

1 shop-bought buckwheat galette

50 g (1¾ oz.) grated cheese (Emmental for a milder taste, Gruyère for a sharper taste)

salt and freshly ground black pepper

FREE FROM
GLUTEN & WHEAT

A FRESH GREEN TWIST TO A FRENCH FAVOURITE, KALE IS A LEAFY AND HEALTHY ADDITION TO AN ALREADY DELICIOUS CREAMY FILLED GALETTE.

1 Heat the olive oil in a frying pan over a medium heat and sauté the kale with a dash of salt and pepper. Set aside.

2 Heat a different frying pan over a medium heat. Place the galette in the pan, add the grated cheese and sautéed kale, and add another dash of freshly ground pepper.

3 When the cheese has melted, remove the galette to a plate and fold in the edges, then serve.

MAKE YOUR OWN BUCKWHEAT GALETTE

IF YOU CAN'T FIND GALETTES IN A SHOP NEAR YOU, YOU CAN TRY MAKING YOUR OWN.

1 Whisk together 240 g (8½ oz.) buckwheat flour, I egg, I20 ml (4 fl oz.) milk, I75 ml (6 fl oz.) water and a pinch of salt. Add the liquids slowly so that the mixture does not become lumpy – you want a smooth, wet batter like melted chocolate.

2 Chill for a few hours in the fridge, then whisk again, adding more water if needed to thin.

3 Heat a frying pan and then add a knob of butter. Fry spoonfuls of the mixture for a few minutes on each side, until golden brown.

CREAMY KALE GALETTE VARIATIONS
THERE ARE MANY DIFFERENT TYPES OF GALETTES. HERE ARE A FEW FUN VARIATIONS TO TRY. DON'T FORGET TO ENJOY THE GALETTE WITH A TRADITIONAL GLASS OF DRY CIDER!

(V) (GF) (WF)

EGG AND KALE GALETTE
While the cheese and kale mix is cooking, crack an egg on top and let it cook. Serve with the egg sunny-side up and the yolk runny.

(V) (GF) (WF)

ONION, POTATO AND CRÈME FRAÎCHE GALETTE
This variation includes just the sautéed kale but adds a delicious twist. Peel and thinly slice 2 small potatoes, then steam in a saucepan with I tablespoon olive oil and some boiling water for about 5–7 minutes. When the potatoes are cooked (you should be able to put a knife through them but do not want them to be overcooked), drain them and add them back to the frying pan. Add I tablespoon olive oil and I–2 thinly sliced shallots and cook for another 5–7 minutes. Add the kale as for the main recipe and continue to sauté until the kale is lightly cooked. Heat a different frying pan over a medium heat. Place the galette in the pan. Add the potato-kale mixture, and a dash of freshly ground black pepper. When the galette is warm, add 2–3 tablespoons of crème fraîche and leave to cook for another 2 minutes. Remove the galette to a plate and fold the edges into a hexagon-type shape. There is no perfect shape so don't worry if the shaping is not exact.

(GF) (WF)

KALE AND HAM GALETTE
For this variation, you can add ham, bacon or lardons to the galette. Cook the meat separately and add at the end.

BUCKWHEAT

Buckwheat, which has its origins in the rhubarb family, is a top gluten-free ingredient. It is also high in fibre and magnesium and has been linked to lowering cholesterol and blood pressure in some studies. Buckwheat is often used to make baked goods, but it can also be used in soups or stews, as a grain in salads, or as a hearty alternative to porridge.

SNACKS, APPETIZERS & DRINKS

PESTO ALFREDO KALE CRISPS

GREEN GUAC-KALE-MOLE

BAKED KALE AND ARTICHOKE DIP

GINGER SHIITAKE AVOCADO SUMMER ROLLS

KALE AND SHIITAKE POT STICKER DUMPLINGS

KALE AND CHORIZO TORTILLA BITES

BABY KALE FALAFEL WITH GREEN HUMMUS

KALE, SWEETCORN AND LEEK FRITTERS

CHEESY KALE AND ARTICHOKE PINWHEELS

KALE DOLMADES

'KALE'SADILLAS

KALE AND CUCUMBER MARGARITA

DIRTY KALE MARTINI

Recipe on page 52

PESTO ALFREDO KALE CRISPS

SERVES	4
PREP	10 minutes, plus soaking
COOK	1 hour 30 minutes

YOU WILL NEED

130 g (4¾ oz.) raw cashew nuts, soaked for several hours

120 ml (4 fl oz.) water, plus more as needed to thin

20 g (¾ oz.) fresh basil

2 garlic cloves, minced

1 tablespoon fresh lemon juice

1 teaspoon sea salt

425 g (15 oz.) kale, washed and de-stemmed

(pictured on page 51)

KALE CRISPS ARE A GREAT HEALTHY ALTERNATIVE TO POTATO CRISPS. HERE, CLASSIC ALFREDO FLAVOURS BRING AN ITALIAN TWIST TO THESE DELICIOUS AND EASY-TO-MAKE SNACKS.

1 Preheat the oven to 110°C/225°F/Gas Mark ½. Line a baking tray with baking paper. If you have a cooling rack, place this on the baking tray to aid the drying process.

2 Combine the soaked cashews with the water in a food processor or liquidizer and blitz on the highest speed until smooth.

3 Add the basil, garlic, lemon juice and salt, and blitz again until smooth. Transfer to a large mixing bowl.

4 Rip the kale into crisp-size pieces. Put in a mixing bowl with the Alfredo pesto. Use your hands to massage the sauce into the kale, coating each piece completely.

5 Arrange the kale in a single layer on the baking tray or rack. Bake for 45 minutes. Remove the tray from the oven, turn the kale over and then bake for another 25–30 minutes, or until the crisps are cooked.

HERE'S A SECRET: This pesto Alfredo kale (uncooked) is also good as a salad with fresh tomatoes thrown in or stirred into freshly cooked pasta.

FREE FROM
DAIRY, GLUTEN & WHEAT

KALE CRISP VARIATIONS

TRY SOME OF THESE FAVOURITE FLAVOUR COMBINATIONS TO FIND YOUR OWN PERFECT MATCH. THE SWEET THAI CHILLI SAUCE CAN ALSO BE USED FOR TOPPING NOODLE BOWLS OR DIPPING POT STICKERS (SEE PAGE 62).

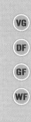

SWEET AND SPICY THAI CRISPS

Combine 100 g (3½ oz.) sugar, 60 ml (2 fl oz.) rice vinegar, 60 ml (2 fl oz.) coconut water, 2 garlic cloves, 1 tablespoon chilli flakes and ½ teaspoon salt in a food processor or liquidizer and blitz on the highest speed until smooth. Coat the kale pieces in the blended mixture and cook as in the main recipe.

SESAME MISO KALE CRISPS

Combine 60 ml (2 fl oz.) smooth miso paste, 1–2 tablespoons olive oil, the juice of 2 lemons and 1 minced spring onion in a food processor or liquidizer and blitz on the highest speed until smooth. Coat the kale pieces in the blended mixture, sprinkle with sesame seeds and cook as in the main recipe.

SALT AND VINEGAR CRISPS

Whisk together 60 ml (2 fl oz.) white or sherry vinegar and 2 tablespoons olive oil in a bowl. Toss the kale pieces in the whisked mixture to coat completely. Sprinkle with sea salt and then cook as in the main recipe.

GREEN GUAC-KALE-MOLE

SERVES	4
PREP	15 minutes

YOU WILL NEED

2 avocados, peeled and stoned

1 or 2 limes

1 teaspoon sea salt

1 tablespoon Worcestershire sauce

50 g (1¾ oz.) kale, washed, de-stemmed and finely chopped

½ red onion, finely diced

200 g (7 oz.) cherry tomatoes, chopped

20 g (¾ oz.) fresh coriander, washed and finely chopped

corn tortilla chips, for serving

THIS KALE-LICIOUS GUACAMOLE IS PACKED WITH ZESTY LIME JUICE. IT PAIRS WELL WITH TORTILLA CHIPS OR IS EVEN GREAT ON TOAST FOR A MORNING OR MIDDAY SNACK.

1 Put the avocado flesh in a bowl and use a fork to mix and mash until you reach a chunky and creamy consistency. Squeeze the juice from half a lime (or I lime, depending on how juicy they are) into the bowl. Add ¼ teaspoon of salt and the Worcestershire sauce, and mix together. Leave the mixture to sit.

2 Put the chopped kale in a separate bowl. Squeeze the juice from another half a lime (or I lime, depending on how juicy they are) into the kale. Add ¼ teaspoon of salt and use your hands to massage the kale, lime juice and salt for 20–30 seconds, then set aside.

3 Add the remaining ingredients to the avocado along with the kale mixture. Add lime juice and the remaining ½ teaspoon of sea salt, taste, and add a little more lime juice or salt if needed.

FREE FROM
DAIRY & WHEAT

BAKED KALE AND ARTICHOKE DIP

(V)

SERVES	12
PREP	10 minutes, plus defrosting
COOK	30 minutes

YOU WILL NEED

250 g (9 oz.) frozen chopped kale, defrosted

250 g (9 oz.) frozen artichokes, defrosted

2 shallots, minced

2 garlic cloves, minced

225 g (8 oz.) cream cheese, at room temperature

280 g (10 oz.) soured cream

1 tablespoon fresh lemon juice

1 teaspoon chopped fresh thyme leaves

pinch of chilli flakes

1 teaspoon fine sea salt

40 g (1½ oz.) grated vegetarian Parmesan cheese

50 g (1¾ oz.) panko or dried breadcrumbs

1 tablespoon olive oil

freshly ground black pepper

cut vegetables, toast, or pita, bagel or corn chips, for serving

HERE'S A TWIST ON THE CLASSIC CROWD PLEASER THAT IS FULL OF DELICIOUS AND NUTRITIOUS KALE.

1 Preheat the oven to 190°C/375°F/Gas Mark 5.

2 Drain any liquid from the kale and artichokes. Put the kale, artichokes, shallots, garlic, cream cheese, soured cream, lemon juice, chilli flakes, salt, a few good grinds of black pepper and half the Parmesan in a food processor fitted with the blade. Process until well combined, then scrape into a 400 ml (14 oz.) casserole dish.

3 Toss the breadcrumbs, the remaining Parmesan and the olive oil together in a small mixing bowl and then sprinkle evenly over the dip. Bake for about 30 minutes in the centre of the oven, until the dip is hot and bubbly and the breadcrumbs are nicely browned.

4 Leave to cool slightly before serving with cut vegetables, small triangles of toast or pita, bagel or corn chips.

NICE AND EASY: Kale from the freezer section works best in this recipe, not only for price and convenience but because freezing and defrosting tenderizes the kale enough so that there's no need to cook it in advance. If you prefer to use fresh, unfrozen kale, boil or steam it until just tender before proceeding with the recipe.

GINGER SHIITAKE AVOCADO SUMMER ROLLS

MAKES	6
PREP	15 minutes

YOU WILL NEED

6 large fresh kale leaves, washed, de-stemmed and chopped

3 tablespoons tahini

6 rice paper wrappers

1 avocado, peeled, pitted and thinly sliced

6 large fresh shiitake mushrooms, sliced

1 cm (½-in.) piece of fresh ginger root, minced

gluten-free soya sauce, for dipping

FLAVOURFUL, FRESH AND PERFECT WITH A SIDE SALAD FOR DINNER OR FOR A COOL LUNCH ON A WARM, SUNNY DAY.

1 First, make sure you have a large plate or surface ready to fill and roll the wrappers on and have your fillings prepped and ready to go. Next, combine the kale with the tahini, making sure the kale is evenly coated.

2 Rehydrate the rice paper wrappers by holding a wrapper under cool running water, getting both sides of the wrapper wet.

3 Remove from the water and, while still firm, place the wrapper on a plate and begin to fill. The rice paper will soften as it sits, but will not be so soft that it sticks to the surface or rips when handling.

4 Place one-sixth of the coated kale in a long row just off-centre of the rice paper wrapper. Add 2–3 avocado slices over the kale and add slices of shiitake mushrooms alongside the avocado. Top with fresh minced ginger.

5 Roll the wrapper up like a burrito – fold the short sides over, then turn and fold one long side over and roll, tuck, roll, tuck, until the filling is completely enclosed.

FREE FROM
DAIRY, GLUTEN & WHEAT

SUMMER ROLL VARIATIONS

THESE CRISPY, CRUNCHY, COLOURFUL VARIATIONS ARE FILLED WITH ESSENTIAL PROTEIN AND VEGGIES. THE SPICY PEANUT NOODLE SPRING ROLLS INCLUDE YOUR FAVOURITE NOODLE BOWL FLAVOURS, ROLLED INTO A PORTABLE MEAL!

SPICY PEANUT NOODLE SPRING ROLLS

Combine 3 tablespoons peanut butter, 55 g (2 oz.) chopped peanuts and I tablespoon hot sauce with I packet (80 g/3 oz.) rice ramen noodles in a bowl. Prepare the rolls as on page 58, adding the kale, avocado and shiitake mushrooms, and then add some of the noodle mixture before rolling to finish.

CASHEW CRUNCH SPRING ROLLS

Prepare the rolls as on page 58, adding the kale, avocado and shiitake mushrooms. Evenly divide 55 g (2 oz.) chopped cashew nuts, yellow pepper slices from I seeded pepper and 2 tablespoons black sesame seeds between the wrappers before rolling.

RAINBOW SPICE ROLL

Prepare the rolls as on page 58, adding the kale, avocado and shiitake mushrooms. Evenly divide matchsticks from half a carrot, red pepper slices from I seeded pepper and 50 g (1¾ oz.) cooked edamame between the wrappers. Drizzle with hot sauce before rolling.

SHIITAKE MUSHROOMS

Shiitake mushrooms are hearty, filling and incredibly flavourful. They can easily replace the meat of a savoury recipe and are much lower in calories than an animal alternative. They are low in sodium and naturally gluten free, as well as being high in healthy antioxidants, vitamin B and potassium. What's more, because shiitakes are plant-based, they are low in cholesterol, too! A very versatile option.

KALE AND SHIITAKE POT STICKER DUMPLINGS (VG)

MAKES	20–25 dumplings
PREP	30 minutes plus draining
COOK	25 minutes

YOU WILL NEED

115 g (4 oz.) kale, washed, de-stemmed and shredded

1 tablespoon salt

groundnut or sunflower oil, for frying

175 g (6 oz.) shiitake mushrooms, diced

1 spring onion, thinly sliced

2 teaspoons fresh ginger root, minced

1 garlic clove, minced

1 tablespoon black rice wine vinegar

2 teaspoons dark soya sauce

1 teaspoon sesame oil

1 teaspoon cornflour

1 teaspoon baking powder

20–25 gyoza wrappers (recipe on page 64)

85 ml (2¾ fl oz.) water

salt and freshly ground black pepper

(continued)

FREE FROM
DAIRY

POT STICKER DUMPLINGS GET THEIR NAME BECAUSE THEY'RE FRIED AND THEN STEAMED IN THE SAME FRYING PAN, GAINING A CRISPY EDGE IN THE PROCESS.

1 Place the kale in a colander. Sprinkle with salt and toss a couple of times to coat it. Put a plate on top of the kale to weigh it down and leave it in the sink to drain for 30 minutes. Rinse with cold water.

2 Warm a little groundnut or sunflower oil in a frying pan. Add the shiitake mushrooms and fry over a medium heat for 3–4 minutes until they're a little browned and any excess liquid has cooked off.

3 Add the kale to the pan. Cook and stir for 3–4 minutes until the kale has wilted a little. Put the mushrooms and kale into a sieve and press with the back of a spoon to squeeze out any excess water. Transfer the mushrooms and kale to a bowl and then season with a good size pinch of salt and pepper.

4 Stir the spring onion, ginger, garlic, black rice wine vinegar, soya sauce, sesame oil, cornflour and baking powder into the mushrooms and kale. Give everything a really good stir to mix it all together.

5 Take one gyoza wrapper and cradle it in the palm of your hand. Add I teaspoon of filling to the middle of it. Fold the wrapper skin over so the edges are lined up and pinch the right hand corner together. Use your right index finger to push a fold into the top (left) side of the wrapper and then pinch the pleat closed with the bottom (right) side of the wrapper. Repeat until you have crimped the top of the dumpling together and have a crescent-shaped dumpling (if you're left handed, just start from the left). Repeat with the rest of the wrappers and filling.

(continued)

3 tablespoons light
soya sauce

1 tablespoon black
rice wine vinegar

2–3 teaspoons chilli oil

pinch of sugar

6 Warm a large, heavy-based frying pan over a medium heat until it's very hot. Add 1–2 tablespoons of groundnut or sunflower oil to the pan and add the dumplings. (If your pan isn't large enough, cook them in batches). Turn the heat down and fry the dumplings for 2–3 minutes until they're golden on the bottom. Add the water to the frying pan, put on the lid and simmer for 10–12 minutes until the water has evaporated and the dumplings are cooked all the way through.

7 Stir the dipping sauce ingredients together and pour them into a bowl. Serve with the hot dumplings.

INGREDIENT SWAP

Black rice wine vinegar has a deep, smoky flavour that matches the earthiness of the mushrooms. If you can't find it, you can use ordinary rice wine vinegar.

MAKE YOUR OWN WRAPPERS (VG) (DF)

MAKING YOUR OWN WRAPPERS IS REALLY EASY — IT JUST TAKES A FEW MINUTES OF KNEADING AND ROLLING. ONCE YOU'VE TRIED DUMPLINGS MADE WITH FRESH DOUGH YOU'LL FIND IT HARD TO GO BACK TO SHOP-BOUGHT WRAPPERS.

1 Sift 155 g (5¼ oz.) plain flour into a large bowl. Slowly pour in 60 ml (2 fl oz.) warm water, mixing it into the flour with a fork or some chopsticks until you have a thick dough. Turn the dough out onto your work surface and knead it for 5–8 minutes until it's smooth — try not to add more flour but keep kneading until it comes together. Put the dough back in the bowl, cover with a clean, damp cloth and leave for 20 minutes while you make the dumpling filling.

2 Turn the dough out and knead again for 5 minutes until smooth. Shape into a log around 2.5 cm (1 in.) wide. Slice 20 rounds off the log. Use a rolling pin to roll each round into a pancake about 7.5–10 cm (3–4 in.) wide. Once they're rolled out, put them on a tray and cover with a clean damp cloth so they don't dry out as you fill and seal them.

FREE FROM
DAIRY

POT STICKER DUMPLING VARIATIONS
ONCE YOU'VE MASTERED THE ART OF SHAPING POT STICKER DUMPLINGS, TRY SWAPPING IN A FEW DIFFERENT STUFFINGS.

PORK AND KALE POT STICKERS
Swap the shiitake mushrooms for 175 g (6 oz.) minced pork. After you've salted the kale, wilt it in a saucepan and drain. Mix all the filling ingredients together and then cook the dumplings as in the main recipe.

PRAWN AND KALE POT STICKERS
De-vein and dice 175 g (6 oz.) cooked prawns. Add them to the rest of the dumpling stuffing mixture with 1 tablespoon oyster sauce. Fill and cook the pot stickers as in the main recipe.

KALE AND CHORIZO TORTILLA BITES

SERVES	8
PREP	15 minutes
COOK	30 minutes

YOU WILL NEED

450 g (1 lb.) potatoes, peeled

125 g (4½ oz.) chorizo, sliced

2 tablespoons olive oil, plus extra for greasing

1 large onion, roughly diced

4 garlic cloves, finely minced

200 g (7 oz.) kale, washed, de-stemmed and roughly chopped

8 eggs, beaten

1 teaspoon smoked paprika

salt and black pepper

salsa or salad, for serving

THIS TASTY SPANISH-STYLE OPEN OMELETTE IS OVEN BAKED FOR EASE. IT'S PERFECT CUT INTO SMALL CUBES TO SERVE TO A CROWD AS AN APPETIZER.

1 Preheat the oven to 200°C/400°F/Gas Mark 6. Grease a large rectangular baking tray or roasting tin with olive oil.

2 Boil the potatoes until just soft, drain and leave to cool before cutting into 2.5 cm (1 in.) pieces.

3 Fry the chorizo in a large frying pan until the oil starts to run and turns golden brown. Remove from the pan and drain on kitchen towel.

4 In the same frying pan, add the olive oil and fry the onion and garlic until soft. Add the kale and continue to cook until it is wilted and soft.

5 In a large bowl, mix the potatoes, chorizo, onion, garlic and kale together, season to taste with salt and black pepper, and spoon the mixture into the prepared baking tray or tin.

6 Add the smoked paprika to the beaten eggs and pour them over the potato mixture. Bake for 25–30 minutes, until the tortilla is set and has puffed up. Leave to cool on the baking tray or roasting tin.

7 To serve as an appetizer or for a buffet, cut into wedges or small cubes and offer cocktail sticks to skewer the tortilla for dipping in salsa. To serve as a meal, cut into larger pieces and serve with fresh salad.

FREE FROM
GLUTEN & WHEAT

BABY KALE FALAFEL WITH GREEN HUMMUS (VG)

SERVES	4
PREP	30 minutes, plus chilling
COOK	30 minutes

FOR THE FALAFEL

240 g (8½ oz.) tinned chickpeas

30 g (1 oz.) baby kale

1 tablespoon sesame seeds

2 garlic cloves, minced

1 teaspoon ground cumin

1 teaspoon ground coriander

pinch of cayenne pepper

2 tablespoons brown rice flour

1 tablespoon extra-virgin olive oil, plus extra for cooking

2 tablespoons water

salt and freshly ground black pepper

salad, wraps and lemon wedges, for serving

FOR THE HUMMUS

80 g (3 oz.) tinned chickpeas

45 g (1½ oz.) baby kale

1 small garlic clove, minced

1½ tablespoons tahini

1 lemon

3 tablespoons extra-virgin olive oil

salt and freshly ground black pepper

SOFT BABY KALE LEAVES HAVE A SHARP, LEMONY FLAVOUR A LITTLE LIKE SORREL OR BABY LEAF SPINACH. THEY GIVE THESE FALAFEL AND HUMMUS A GORGEOUS GREEN COLOUR.

1 Start by making the falafel. Drain and rinse the chickpeas and place in a food processor or liquidizer. Add the baby kale, sesame seeds, garlic, spices with a pinch of salt and the brown rice flour. Pour in the extra-virgin olive oil and water and pulse until you have a chunky paste. Add extra water if the mixture seems too dry and crumbly.

2 Scoop the falafel mixture out of the processor and shape into 12 flattish, round patties. Put them on a plate, cover with cling film and chill for 1 hour or overnight.

3 To make the hummus, tip the chickpeas into a food processor. Add the baby kale, garlic and tahini. Finely grate the zest from the lemon and add it to the hummus along with the juice of the lemon and the extra-virgin olive oil.

4 Pulse the hummus until it's smooth and thick. If it seems too dry, add more olive oil or a splash of water. Taste and season with salt and pepper and put to one side.

5 Preheat the oven to 180°C/350°F/Gas Mark 4. Grease a baking tray with a little olive oil. Arrange the falafel on the tray and bake for 30 minutes, turning them after 15 minutes, until they are golden brown and cooked through.

6 Warm 4 wraps in the bottom of the oven for the final 1–2 minutes to soften them. Serve the falafel in the wraps with salad, spoonfuls of the green hummus and lemon wedges for squeezing.

FREE FROM
DAIRY

KALE, SWEETCORN AND LEEK FRITTERS

(V)

MAKES	20 small fritters
PREP	15 minutes
COOK	40 minutes

YOU WILL NEED

2 tablespoons olive oil

2 leeks, trimmed, halved lengthways and thinly sliced

¾ teaspoon fine sea salt

2 garlic cloves, minced

450 g (1 lb.) cavolo nero, washed, de-stemmed and torn into bite-size pieces

300 g (10½ oz.) sweetcorn kernels, thawed if frozen

30 g (1 oz.) finely chopped fresh flat-leaf parsley

20 g (¾ oz.) grated vegetarian Parmesan cheese

1 tablespoon fresh lemon juice

¼ teaspoon dried dill

2 eggs

120 ml (4 fl oz.) buttermilk

60 g (2¼ oz.) plain flour

75 g (2½ oz.) polenta

¼ teaspoon bicarbonate of soda

vegetable oil, for frying

black pepper

soured cream, for serving (optional)

THESE ADAPTABLE FRIED CAKES MAKE A GREAT HORS D'OEUVRE FOR A CASUAL COCKTAIL PARTY, A GOOD SCHOOL LUNCH, OR EVEN AN EXCELLENT DINNER WITH A FRIED EGG ON TOP.

1 In a large non-stick frying pan, heat the olive oil over a medium-high heat. Add the leeks and a sprinkle of the salt and cook for about 7 minutes, stirring occasionally, until softened. Adjust the heat as necessary to prevent browning. Add the garlic and cook, stirring, for 1 minute. Add the kale and cook for about 5 minutes, stirring frequently, until wilted and tender.

2 Transfer the contents of the frying pan to a mixing bowl and stir in the sweetcorn, parsley, Parmesan, lemon juice, dill and the remaining salt. Season with black pepper. Create a well in the centre of the bowl, crack in the eggs and beat well. Pour in the buttermilk and stir.

3 Sprinkle the flour, polenta and bicarbonate of soda over the top and mix gently until combined.

4 Wipe out the frying pan, add a thin layer of oil and heat over a medium-high heat until shimmering. Spoon 2–3 tablespoons of batter into the frying pan for each cake, working in batches without crowding the pan. Reduce the heat to medium-low and adjust as necessary so the cakes cook through without burning. Cook for about 4 minutes per side so that they are golden brown.

5 Set the cooked cakes on a wire rack or kitchen towel–lined plate. Add a little more oil to the pan and continue cooking in batches until you've used all the batter. Serve warm or at room temperature, with a dollop of soured cream, if desired.

MAKE AHEAD: These fritters are incredibly versatile and can be made in advance and then reheated or served at room temperature.

CHEESY KALE AND ARTICHOKE PINWHEELS (VG)

SERVES	4
PREP	30 minutes, plus chilling
COOK	30 minutes

YOU WILL NEED

70 g (2½ oz.) kale, washed, de-stemmed and chopped

1 tablespoon nutritional yeast

1 tablespoon olive oil

125 g (4½ oz.) marinated artichoke hearts, chopped

1 garlic clove, minced

35 g (1¼ oz.) canned water chestnuts, chopped

1 gluten-free puff pastry sheet (half a packet, approximately 500 g/ 1 lb. 2 oz.), thawed

THESE FANCY, COLOURFUL PASTRIES ARE FULL OF FLAVOUR AND WILL BE THE FIRST THING TO DISAPPEAR AT ANY PARTY. YOU CAN MAKE THESE FOR LUNCH BY SUBSTITUTING THE PUFF PASTRY WITH LARGE TORTILLAS.

ADVANCE PREPARATION: You will need to allow several hours for this to set before baking, or prepare the day before baking.

1 Combine the kale, nutritional yeast, olive oil, artichoke hearts, garlic and water chestnuts in a mixing bowl.

2 Roll the puff pastry sheet into a 28 x 35 cm (11 x 14 in.) rectangle. Leaving a 2.5 cm (1 in.) border on one long side, spread the filling all over the puff pastry.

3 Beginning at the long side without a border, carefully roll the pastry and press together to seal the edge at the border. Wrap in cling film and refrigerate for at least 4 hours before baking.

4 When ready to bake, preheat the oven to 180°C/350°F/Gas Mark 4 and line a baking tray with baking paper.

5 Unwrap the pastry from the cling film and slice it into 1 cm (½ in.) rounds. Place on the baking tray, spaced 1 cm (½ in). apart. Bake for 15–17 minutes until golden brown. Serve warm.

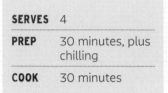

FREE FROM
DAIRY, GLUTEN & WHEAT

KALE PINWHEEL VARIATIONS
FLAKY PASTRY PINWHEELS ARE THE PERFECT HOME FOR RICH AND BRINY PROVENÇAL TAPENADE, CROWD-PLEASING PIZZA FLAVOURS OR THE SURPRISING COMBINATION OF APRICOT AND ROSEMARY — LIKE SUMMER AND AUTUMN IN ONE BITE!

KALAMATA TAPENADE PINWHEELS
Combine the kale, nutritional yeast and olive oil in a mixing bowl as on page 72. Omit the artichokes, garlic and water chestnuts and in their place add 30 g (1 oz.) kalamata olives, 30 g (1 oz.) pine nuts and 40 g (1½ oz.) capers, and continue with the main recipe.

PIZZA PINWHEELS
Combine the kale, nutritional yeast and olive oil in a mixing bowl as on page 72. Substitute the artichokes, garlic and water chestnuts with 30 g (1 oz.) chopped sun-dried tomatoes, half a seeded and chopped green pepper and 55 g (2 oz.) roasted cashew nuts, chopped, and continue with the main recipe.

SWEET AND SAVOURY APRICOT AND ROSEMARY PINWHEELS
Combine the kale, nutritional yeast and olive oil in a mixing bowl as on page 72. Instead of the artichokes, garlic and water chestnuts, add 160 g (5½ oz.) dried apricots, 2 de-stemmed and chopped fresh rosemary sprigs, 80 g (3 oz.) roasted cashew nuts, chopped, and 50 g (1¾ oz.) light soft brown sugar, and continue with the main recipe.

ARTICHOKES

Artichokes offer a unique, tangy flavour to savoury dishes. They are packed with vitamins, fibre and antioxidants, and are fun to eat. The tender petals are deliciously dippable, but the best part of the artichoke is the juicy heart. The centre of this superfood is extremely versatile, adding flavour to all kinds of dishes. Keeping a jar or tin of good-quality marinated artichokes in the cupboard makes it easy to liven up salads or pasta by adding a few.

KALE DOLMADES

(VG)

SERVES	6–8
PREP	30 minutes
COOK	50 minutes

YOU WILL NEED

extra-virgin olive oil,
   for frying

1 small onion, diced

150 g (5¼ oz.) long-grain
   white rice

50 g (1¼ oz.) currants

375 g (13 oz.) boiling
   water, plus an
   additional 120 ml
   (4 fl oz.) hot water

50 g (1¼ oz.) pine nuts

big handful of fresh
   parsley, chopped

small handful of fresh
   dill, chopped

small handful of fresh
   mint, leaves chopped

1 teaspoon ground
   cinnamon

1 tablespoon tomato
   purée

juice of 1 lemon

600 g (1 lb. 5 oz.) cavolo
   nero

salt and black pepper

fresh salad and lemon
   slices, for serving

FREE FROM
DAIRY, GLUTEN
& WHEAT

LIKE VINE LEAVES, LONG, FLAT CAVOLO NERO LEAVES ARE GREAT FOR STUFFING. THESE DELICIOUS DOLMADES ARE PERFECT AS PART OF A MEZE MEAL.

1 Warm a little extra-virgin olive oil in a saucepan over a low heat. Add the onion and season with salt and pepper. Place the lid on the saucepan and gently cook for 10 minutes, until the onion is soft but not coloured. Stir every so often.

2 Stir the rice and currants into the saucepan. Pour in the boiling water, cover, turn up the heat and bring to a boil. Turn the heat down and simmer for 10 minutes until the rice is cooked and all the water has been absorbed.

3 While the rice is cooking, warm a dry frying pan over a medium heat. Add the pine nuts and toast for 2–3 minutes, shaking the pan constantly, until the nuts are golden and smell nutty.

4 Add the pine nuts to the rice with the freshly chopped herbs, cinnamon, tomato purée and lemon juice. Stir together, taste, and add salt and pepper if you think it needs it. Put to one side.

5 While the filling is cooking, fill a large saucepan with more water and bring to a boil. Add the cavolo nero to the saucepan, simmer for 2 minutes to just soften it and then drain well.

6 Place a cavolo nero leaf, stem side up, on your work surface. Place 1 tablespoon of the filling in the middle of the leaf. Fold the stem up over the filling, fold the sides over the middle, and then roll up the dolmade starting from the stem end. Place seam side down on a plate and continue filling and rolling the rest of the dolmades.

7 Nestle the dolmades in a wide, heavy-based saucepan. Pour in 120 ml (4 fl oz.) hot water. Cover and cook over a medium heat for 25–30 minutes until the water has simmered off. These are best served warm or cold rather than piping hot from the saucepan.

'KALE'SADILLAS

(V)

SERVES	I
PREP	I5 minutes
COOK	I5 minutes

YOU WILL NEED

1 tablespoon olive oil
½ red pepper, diced
50 g (1¾ oz.) kale,
    washed, de-stemmed
    and roughly chopped
1–2 spring onions, diced
1 tortilla
½ tin (200 g/7 oz.)
    refried beans
    (optional)
50 g (1¾ oz.) grated
    cheddar cheese
handful of fresh
    coriander, washed and
    chopped
salsa and soured cream,
    for serving

QUESADILLAS ARE REALLY EASY TO MAKE AND TURN AN ORDINARY LUNCH INTO A FUN EVENT. MULTIPLY THE RECIPE IF YOU INTEND TO SHARE!

1 Add the olive oil to a saucepan over a medium heat. Sauté the pepper, kale and spring onions together for 5–7 minutes.

2 Put the tortilla in a separate dry frying pan over a medium heat and spread the beans over the top, if using.

3 After I–2 minutes of the beans cooking, add the vegetable mixture, cheese and coriander.

4 Fold the tortilla in half. Cook for another 2 minutes and then flip. Cook for another 3–4 minutes and flip again until the cheese begins to melt. Serve with salsa and soured cream.

KALE AND CUCUMBER MARGARITA

KALE CAN BE A SURPRISINGLY DELICIOUS ADDITION TO HAPPY HOUR! ENJOY A SPLASH OF KALE JUICE IN YOUR COCKTAIL TO ADD A FEW EXTRA VITAMINS TO YOUR EVENING.

SERVES	1
PREP	10 minutes

YOU WILL NEED

90 ml (3 fl oz.) cucumber juice

20–45 ml (¾–1½ fl oz.) kale juice

90 ml (3 fl oz.) lime juice, plus extra for the rim of the glass

rock salt, for the rim

ice

45–90 ml (1½–3 fl oz.) tequila

20 ml (¾ fl oz.) simple syrup

cucumber slices and lime wedges, for serving

1 First make the cucumber juice. Feed about half a cucumber through a juicer according to the manufacturer's instructions. Juicer yields vary, so you may use more or less cucumber depending on your needs.

2 Make the kale juice as above, using about 5 leaves of kale (including stems).

3 Now salt the rim of the glass. Pour some lime juice into a shallow dish and the rock salt into another (you'll need enough to cover the bottom of the dish). Turn your glass upside down and dip into the juice and then into the salt.

4 Fill the cocktail glass with ice. In a cocktail shaker or jar with a lid, combine the cucumber juice, kale juice, remaining lime juice, tequila and simple syrup and mix well. Pour over the ice in the glass and serve with a wedge of lime or slice of cucumber.

FREE FROM
DAIRY, GLUTEN & WHEAT

KALE COCKTAIL VARIATIONS
YOU MIGHT BE SURPRISED, BUT KALE JUICE WORKS WELL IN MOST OF YOUR FAVOURITE BOOZY DRINKS.

(VG) (DF) (GF) (WF)

ELDERFLOWER AND KALE SPRITZER
Fill a wine glass with 3–4 ice cubes and fill up two-thirds of the way with sparkling water. Add 20 ml (¾ fl oz.) kale juice, 20–45 ml (¾–1½ fl oz.) elderflower liqueur (Saint Germain is a good brand) and 45 ml (1½ fl oz.) cucumber juice. Serve with a slice of lemon. Serves I.

(VG) (DF) (GF) (WF)

KALE GIN FIZZ
Fill a tumbler with ice and half fill with sparkling water. Add 90 ml (3 fl oz.) cucumber juice, 45 ml (1½ fl oz.) kale juice, 45 ml (1½ fl oz.) gin and 45 ml (1½ fl oz.) simple syrup and stir to mix. Serve with a slice of cucumber on the rim of the glass. Serves I.

(VG) (DF) (GF) (WF)

KALE GRANITA
Blend about 16 ice cubes, 180 ml (6 fl oz.) rum or cachaça (Brazilian liqueur), 2–3 slices of fresh or tinned and drained pineapple, 90 ml (3 fl oz.) cucumber juice, 45 ml (1½ fl oz.) kale juice and 45 ml (1½ fl oz.) simple syrup in a liquidizer until the ice is crushed. Add more or less alcohol to taste. Serves 3–4.

CUCUMBERS

Cucumbers, which originate from Southeast Asia, are 90 per cent water and contain silica, which is amazing for the skin. They contain high levels of potassium, magnesium and vitamins C and K. Juicing them is a refreshing way to reap their nutritional benefits.

Cucumber, lime juice and mint make for a refreshing twist on old-fashioned lemonade. Why not try it with a little kale juice too?

DIRTY KALE MARTINI

(VG)

MAKES	I
PREP	5 minutes

YOU WILL NEED

80 ml (2¾ fl oz.) gin

15 ml (½ fl oz.) dry vermouth

15 ml (½ fl oz.) fresh kale juice

15 ml (½ fl oz.) olive juice (from the jar)

5–10 ml (¼ fl oz.) fresh lemon juice

olives, for garnish

SOMETIMES IT'S FUN TO CHANGE THINGS A LITTLE. LEMON AND OLIVE PAIR PERFECTLY WITH BOTH GIN AND KALE, AND THIS MARTINI MARRIES THESE INGREDIENTS TO CREATE A BALANCED AND FLAVOURFUL COCKTAIL.

1 First make the kale juice. Feed about 5 large kale leaves (including stems) through a juicer according to the manufacturer's instructions. Juicer yields vary greatly, especially for leafy greens, so you may need a couple more or fewer leaves.

2 Pour the gin, vermouth, kale juice, olive juice and lemon juice into a mixing glass or jar filled with ice. Stir and strain into a chilled cocktail glass. Garnish with olives and serve immediately.

FREE FROM
DAIRY, GLUTEN & WHEAT

Recipe on page 91

MAIN COURSES

SAUSAGE STEW WITH KALE AND LENTILS

WHITE BEAN AND KALE PORTOBELLO BURGERS

PIZZA WITH KALE AND TALEGGIO

SPICY CHIPOTLE, KALE AND LIME ENCHILADAS

KALE, BACON AND EGG RICE BOWL

TAIWANESE PORK BELLY BUNS WITH PICKLED KALE

STUFFED SWEET POTATOES WITH KALE,
BLACK BEANS AND CHIPOTLE CASHEW CREAM

KALE, PARMESAN AND LEMON PEARL BARLEY RISOTTO

LENTILS, CARAMELIZED ONIONS AND KALE WITH ROASTED WALNUTS

KALE AND SWEET POTATO DOSAS WITH COCONUT CHUTNEY

SAUSAGE STEW WITH KALE AND LENTILS

SERVES	4
PREP	30 minutes, plus chilling
COOK	1 hour

YOU WILL NEED

extra-virgin olive oil, for frying

450 g (1 lb.) pork sausages

1 large onion, diced

1 large leek, trimmed and finely sliced

2 carrots, peeled and diced

1 celery stick, diced

2 garlic cloves, minced

240 g (8½ oz.) cooked green lentils

2 fresh thyme sprigs

1 dried bay leaf

650 ml (22 fl oz.) hot chicken stock

450 g (1 lb.) kale, washed and de-stemmed

salt and black pepper

FREE FROM DAIRY

A WARMING STEW CAN MAKE YOU GLAD FOR COLD, WINTRY DAYS. THIS ITALIAN-STYLE SAUSAGE STEW IS GREAT BY ITSELF, BUT YOU COULD ALSO SERVE SOME CRUSTY BREAD ON THE SIDE TO MOP UP THE JUICES.

1 Warm a splash of extra-virgin olive oil in a deep frying pan or wok over medium-low heat. Add the sausages and fry for 4–5 minutes, turning the sausages so they are browned all over. Lift the sausages out of the pan and leave to rest on a plate.

2 Add the onion, leek, carrot and celery to the frying pan and season with salt and pepper. Sauté for 8–10 minutes until the vegetables have softened. If they look like they are starting to stick to the bottom of the pan, add a splash of water.

3 Stir the garlic into the vegetable mixture. Cook, and stir for 1 minute, until the frying pan smells sweet and aromatic. Stir in the lentils, thyme and bay leaf.

4 Add the sausages back to the frying pan, nestling them among the vegetables. Pour in the hot chicken stock. Cover and simmer over a low heat for 30 minutes until the sausages are cooked through.

5 Add the kale to the frying pan. Stir for about 5–8 minutes until the kale has wilted and is just cooked. Taste and adjust the seasoning and then serve immediately.

BRAISED SAUSAGE AND KALE VARIATIONS
SAUSAGES, LENTILS AND KALE GO TOGETHER SO WELL, BUT YOU DON'T HAVE TO STICK WITH ITALIAN SEASONINGS. MIX THINGS UP WITH SOME NORTH AFRICAN SPICE OR TRY A DIFFERENT MEAT FOR A LIGHTER FLAVOUR.

MERGUEZ SAUSAGES BRAISED WITH KALE AND LENTILS
Swap the pork sausages for 450 g (I lb.) merguez sausages, and the thyme and bay for 2 teaspoons cumin seeds and I teaspoon chilli flakes. Merguez sausages are normally thinner than pork sausages, so reduce the cooking time in step 4 to 20–25 minutes. Scatter with plenty of chopped fresh parsley for serving.

CHICKEN STEW WITH KALE AND LENTILS
Instead of sausages, brown 4 chicken thighs and 4 drumsticks. Carry on with the recipe on page 88, but allow 40–45 minutes for cooking in step 4. Keep your eye on the pan and add a splash of water if you think the chicken is drying out too quickly.

SAUSAGE STEW WITH KALE AND CHICKPEAS
Fry the sausages over a low heat for I0–12 minutes, until cooked through. Swap the onion and leek for 2 diced red onions, the lentils for 240 g (8½ oz.) cooked chickpeas, and the thyme and bay leaf for a handful of chopped fresh sage and a diced mild red chilli. Follow the recipe, but reduce the cooking time in step 4 to 20–25 minutes. Crumble a little feta cheese over the dish before serving.

WHITE BEAN AND KALE PORTOBELLO BURGERS (VG)

SERVES	2
PREP	10 minutes
COOK	35 minutes

YOU WILL NEED

2 large portobello mushrooms

1 tablespoon olive oil

1 small sweet onion, peeled and chopped

2 garlic cloves, minced

175 g (6 oz.) cooked white beans, such as haricot beans, mashed

4 large kale leaves, washed, de-stemmed and chopped into small pieces

2 large gluten-free burger buns

kale leaves, tomato slices, avocado slices, and tomato salsa (optional), for serving

(pictured on page 86)

FREE FROM
DAIRY, GLUTEN & WHEAT

THESE DELICIOUSLY HEARTY BURGERS ARE A FAVOURITE IN ANY HOUSEHOLD AND WILL BE REQUESTED AGAIN AND AGAIN.

1 Preheat the oven to 180°C/350°F/Gas Mark 4 and line a baking tray with baking paper.

2 Clean the mushrooms using kitchen towel and remove the stems. With a sharp spoon, scrape the gills out of each mushroom and discard. Place the portobello caps on the baking tray, stem side down.

3 Bake in the oven for 10 minutes to remove excess liquid. Remove from the oven and set aside to cool.

4 Heat the olive oil in a saucepan over a medium heat, then add the onion, garlic, beans and kale, and sauté for about 10 minutes, until soft.

5 Fill each portobello cap with the kale and bean mixture and place on the baking tray. Bake for 15 minutes. Serve on a toasted bun with kale leaves, tomato slices and avocado slices, with salsa on the side, if desired.

PIZZA WITH KALE AND TALEGGIO

(V)

MAKES	two 12-inch (30 cm) pizzas
PREP	20 minutes, plus proofing
COOK	10 minutes

YOU WILL NEED

450 g (1 lb.) ball regular, wholewheat or multigrain pizza dough

plain flour, for dusting

450 g (1 lb.) kale, washed and de-stemmed

60 ml (2 fl oz.) olive oil

1 tablespoon fresh lemon juice

4 garlic cloves

¼ teaspoon salt

¼ teaspoon chilli flakes

40 g (1½ oz.) grated vegetarian Pecorino Romano cheese

12 black Moroccan oil-cured olives, pitted

300 g (10½ oz.) Taleggio cheese

WHEN COOKED IN A VERY HOT OVEN, KALE BECOMES CHARRED AND CRISPY IN PLACES, LENDING A NUTTY, SLIGHTLY SMOKY AND UTTERLY DELICIOUS FLAVOUR TO THIS PIZZA.

1 Preheat the oven to 290°C/550°F/Gas Mark 10, or as high as it will go, and place a rack in the top third of the oven. If you have a pizza stone, set it on the rack. Let the oven preheat, so it's as hot as it can be.

2 Divide the dough into two balls, flour lightly and set aside on a cutting board covered with a clean cloth or towel. Let the dough rest for at least 30 minutes.

3 If using cavolo nero, cut the leaves into long, thin strips. If using curly kale, tear the leaves into large, uneven pieces.

4 Pour 2 tablespoons of the olive oil and the lemon juice into a large mixing bowl. Smash the garlic cloves on a cutting board, peel off the skins and sprinkle with the salt. Using a chef's knife, mince the garlic with the salt until it turns into a rough paste. Place half the salted garlic into the mixing bowl, whisk the dressing together with a fork, and then add the kale. Using your hands, massage the dressing into the kale for 1–2 minutes. Set aside to rest.

5 In a small bowl, combine the remaining 2 tablespoons of olive oil, the remaining salted garlic and the chilli flakes.

6 If using a pizza stone, line a pizza peel with a 30 cm (12 in.) square of baking paper. On the paper, shape one piece of dough into a thin 30 cm (12 in.) circle. A 'rustic' circle is totally acceptable! Brush with half the garlic–chilli oil, working all the way to the edges. Sprinkle on 2 tablespoons of the Pecorino. Tear six of the olives into pieces and scatter across the dough. Cut the Taleggio into small pieces – you can include or not include the rind based on your preference – and scatter almost half the pieces across the dough, reserving a few.

(continued)

RICOTTA CHEESE
Ricotta cheese adds creaminess and is a great contrast to crispy pizza base, see variation on page 95.

7 Slide the pizza and the baking paper off the peel onto the stone. Bake until risen and lightly golden, about 5 minutes, then remove from the oven using the peel. Working quickly, scatter half the dressed kale onto the pizza and top with the few reserved pieces of Taleggio. Return to oven and bake for 5 minutes more. For the final minute, turn the grill on high. The crust should be nicely browned in spots and the kale lightly charred. Remove the pizza from the oven, cut into slices and serve. Repeat the process to make a second pizza.

NO STONE, NO PROBLEM: To cook the pizza without a stone, place a baking tray in the hot oven at least half an hour before baking. Prepare the pizza on a sheet of baking paper and carefully slide the uncooked pizza onto the hot tray. Bake as directed.

KALE PIZZA VARIATIONS

HAVING A FEW SPECIAL PIZZA RECIPES UNDER YOUR BELT GIVES YOU 'COOL' POINTS AS BOTH A FAMILY DINNER PLANNER AND A PARTY HOST. ADD THESE VARIATIONS TO YOUR REPERTOIRE AND YOUR STREET CRED WILL SKYROCKET.

CREAMY RICOTTA AND CHERRY TOMATO PIZZA

To add a layer of creaminess, brush plain olive oil onto the crust and mix the garlic, chilli flakes and Pecorino with 335 g (11¾ oz.) ricotta cheese. Spread evenly over the pizza crusts or dollop in spots under and over the kale. Add 250 g (9 oz.) halved cherry tomatoes to the pizza before placing in the oven. Include or omit the olives and Taleggio as desired.

KALE SALAD PIZZA

For a fresh and equally delicious twist on this pizza, use cavolo nero and cut into very thin ribbons. Toss with the dressing as indicated above, but do not bake. Simply add the kale salad to the top of the pizza before serving.

GOOD OLD CHEESE PIZZA WITH KALE

Garlicky kale that's tender in spots and smoky charred in others works equally well on a classic cheese pizza. To make this version, halve the olive oil, garlic and salt. Make the kale dressing as directed, but don't make any chilli oil. Instead, ladle about 120 ml (4 fl oz.) of your favourite tomato sauce onto the crust and spread evenly, leaving a thin border around the edge. Replace the Taleggio with grated mozzarella. Omit the olives. Bake as directed in the main recipe.

SPICY CHIPOTLE, KALE AND LIME ENCHILADAS (VG)

SERVES	6
PREP	15 minutes
COOK	30 minutes

YOU WILL NEED

1 tablespoon olive oil

1 small onion, diced

1 garlic clove, minced

3–4 tinned chipotle peppers in adobo, diced

1 tin (794 g/26 oz.) finely chopped tomatoes

450 g (1 lb.) kale, washed, de-stemmed and chopped

240 g (8½ oz.) cooked brown rice

280 g (9¾ oz.) cooked black beans

6 wholewheat tortillas

salt and black pepper

FOR THE LIME CASHEW CREAM

130 g (4¾ oz.) raw cashew nuts, soaked for several hours

juice and grated zest of 2 limes (about 120 ml/4 fl. oz. juice)

120 ml (4 fl. oz.) water, as needed

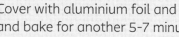

FREE FROM DAIRY

NOTHING SAYS COMFORT FOOD LIKE A BIG DISH OF ENCHILADAS — THE LIME CASHEW CREAM JUST SENDS THESE OVER THE TOP!

1 First, make the lime cashew cream. Combine the soaked cashews with the lime juice and zest in a food processor or liquidizer and blitz on the highest speed until smooth. Add water by the tablespoon to thin to the desired consistency. Set aside until needed (this will keep in the fridge for up to 3 days).

2 Preheat the oven to 180°C/350°F/Gas Mark 4.

3 Heat the olive oil in a large saucepan over a medium heat, and sauté the onion and garlic until translucent.

4 Add the chipotle, tomatoes and kale, and simmer for 10–15 minutes, stirring occasionally. Remove from the heat and season with salt and pepper to taste.

5 Transfer two-thirds of the sauce to a large bowl and add the cooked rice and beans. Reserve the remaining one-third of the sauce to top the enchiladas.

6 Assemble the enchiladas: warm the tortillas in a dry frying pan over a low heat or for a few seconds in the microwave.

7 Spoon a few tablespoons of the reserved sauce into the bottom of a baking dish. Place ⅔ cup of the rice and beans mixture into the middle of a tortilla and top with 3–4 tablespoons of the lime cashew cream.

8 Roll up the tortilla and place it seam side down in the baking dish. Repeat with the other 5 tortillas and then pour the remaining reserved sauce over the top.

9 Cover with aluminium foil and bake for 30 minutes. Remove the foil and bake for another 5-7 minutes.

KALE, BACON AND EGG RICE BOWL

SERVES	1
PREP	10 minutes
COOK	30 minutes

YOU WILL NEED

60 g (2¼ oz.) brown basmati rice

1 tablespoon rice wine vinegar

1 tablespoon sesame seeds

1 egg

75 g (2½ oz.) kale, washed, de-stemmed and shredded

180 ml (6 fl oz.) boiling water to cover the kale

3 rashers of bacon

sriracha or other hot sauce, for serving

FREE FROM DAIRY, GLUTEN & WHEAT

GRAIN BOWLS MAKE A HEALTHY, COMFORTING MEAL. THIS ONE FEATURES NUTTY BROWN BASMATI RICE TOPPED WITH KALE, CRISP BACON AND A SOFTLY POACHED EGG.

1 Rinse the rice under cold running water for a minute or two. If you have time, soak it in cold water for up to 30 minutes, then rinse it well.

2 Add the rice to a saucepan. Cover with the boiling water, put on the lid and bring to a boil. As soon as it is boiling, turn the heat down as low as possible and let the rice gently simmer for about 25 minutes until all the water has been absorbed.

3 Take the rice off the heat and leave it in the saucepan with the lid on for 5 minutes more. Stir the vinegar and sesame seeds into the rice.

4 Fill a deep frying pan with water around 6 cm (2½ in.) deep. Bring it just to a boil, so a few bubbles are breaking the surface. Crack the egg into a cup or bowl and slip it into the water.

5 Let the egg cook gently for 1 minute – the water should bubble lightly. Remove from the heat and let the egg sit in the water for 3–5 minutes until it is cooked to your liking. If some of the egg is raised out of the water, spoon hot water over it occasionally.

6 While the egg poaches, put the kale in a heatproof bowl. Cover with boiling water, leave for 2 minutes and then drain well.

7 Grill the bacon until crisp. Spoon the rice into a warm serving bowl and top with the kale and bacon. Lift the poached egg out of the water with a slotted spoon, place on top and serve with hot sauce.

TAIWANESE PORK BELLY BUNS WITH PICKLED KALE

MAKES	12 buns
PREP	45 minutes, plus rising, proofing, pickling and marinating
COOK	3 hours 30 minutes

FOR THE PORK BELLY

85 g (3 oz.) light soft brown sugar

2 star anise

1 tablespoon fresh ginger root, minced

2 garlic cloves, minced

60 ml (2 fl oz.) boiling water

900 g (2 lb.) pork belly

groundnut or sunflower oil, for frying

FOR THE BUNS

110 ml (3¾ fl oz.) milk

120 ml (4 fl oz.) water

4 teaspoons dried yeast

2 teaspoons sugar

450 g (1 lb.) bread flour, plus a little extra for dusting

2 teaspoons baking powder

1 teaspoon bicarbonate of soda

1 teaspoon salt

vegetable oil, for greasing

(continued)

GUA BAO ARE THE FLUFFY STEAMED BUNS POPULAR IN STREET FOOD MARKETS AROUND THE WORLD. THERE ARE A FEW STEPS INVOLVED TO MAKE THEM AT HOME, BUT NONE ARE TOO DIFFICULT.

THE DAY BEFORE

1 In a bowl, mix together all of the pork belly ingredients except for the pork and oil, stirring until the sugar has dissolved. Put the pork belly in a dish then spread the marinade over both sides. Leave the pork to marinate in the mixture for 1 hour.

2 Preheat the oven to 250°C/500°F/Gas Mark 9. Shake off the pork belly and place in a roasting tin, reserving the marinade. Roast for 30 minutes to blister the skin.

3 Spoon the leftover marinade over the pork. Cover the dish loosely with aluminium foil, turn the oven down to 150°C/300°F/Gas Mark 2 and roast for 2 hours, until the pork is cooked all the way through but isn't falling apart. Take the pork out of the oven and leave to cool in the tin. Wrap tightly in foil and chill overnight in the fridge.

A FEW HOURS BEFORE

4 Start making the buns. Warm the milk and water together in a saucepan until they are just hand hot, and then sprinkle in the yeast and sugar. Remove the saucepan from the heat and let sit until the yeast has been activated and there is plenty of froth on top of the liquid.

5 Sift the remaining ingredients into a large bowl. Pour in the warm milk and water and stir together with your hand until it forms a dough. Turn it out onto your work surface and knead for 8–10 minutes until the dough is silky and smooth. If it sticks a little, just keep kneading. Try not to add extra flour, as that will dry out the dough. Put the dough back in the bowl, cover with a clean cloth, and leave in a warm spot for 2 hours until the dough has doubled in size.

(continued)

FOR THE PICKLED KALE

200 g (7 oz.) kale, washed, de-stemmed and shredded

120 ml (4 fl oz.) white wine vinegar

65 g (2½ oz.) sugar

2 teaspoons salt

FOR THE GARNISHES

140 g (5 oz.) raw peanuts

2 tablespoons water

2 tablespoons sugar

1 tablespoon Chinese five-spice powder

1 teaspoon salt

fresh coriander, shredded spring onions and sliced chillies, for serving

6 While the dough is rising, pickle the kale. In a large bowl, cover the kale with boiling water and soak for 2 minutes. Drain it and squeeze out any excess water.

7 Mix the rest of the kale ingredients together in a bowl. Stir in the kale, cover, and let sit for at least I hour or overnight.

8 Make the peanut garnish now, too. Toast the peanuts in a dry frying pan for 3–4 minutes, shaking the pan, until they are golden all over. Turn them into a bowl and rub off and discard the skins.

9 Add the water and sugar to the same frying pan. Bubble for I–2 minutes until syrupy, then stir in the peanuts and the remaining ingredients. Turn the peanuts out onto a board, roughly chop, and put to one side for later.

WHEN READY TO SERVE

10 Turn out the dough onto your work surface and punch it a couple of times to knock it back. Divide it into 12 equal pieces. Dust your work surface with a little flour and roll out each piece of dough until it's 10 cm (4 in.) wide. Place on a tray or board, cover with a clean cloth or towel, and leave to prove for 30 minutes.

11 Once the buns look puffy and have risen, grease a chopstick with a little vegetable oil, place it in the middle of each bun, and fold it over. Set the oven to its lowest setting.

12 Line a flat steamer basket with baking paper. Place it in a saucepan or wok with a few inches of simmering water in the bottom. Steam the buns in batches for 10–15 minutes per batch until they are light and fluffy. Keep them warm in the oven.

13 Slice the pork belly into pieces around 5 mm (¼ in.) thick. Warm the oil in a frying pan and fry the pork belly slices in batches for 5–6 minutes, turning a few times, until crisp and caramelized. Once cooked, slice each piece in half. Put the cooked pork belly on a plate and keep warm in the oven.

14 Put the pickled kale, the peanuts, some fresh coriander leaves, a few sliced spring onions and sliced chillies in little bowls to go on the table so people can help themselves.

15 Take the buns and pork belly to the table and let everyone assemble their own perfect buns and pickled kale.

TAIWANESE BUN VARIATIONS
PORK BELLY IS THE CLASSIC FILLING IN STEAMED TAIWANESE BUNS, BUT THERE ARE LOTS OF WAYS TO MIX THINGS UP. THEY NEEDN'T BE OFF-LIMITS TO VEGETARIANS OR VEGANS EITHER.

STEAK, MUSTARD SAUCE AND PICKLED KALE

Make the kale and buns as per the recipe. On the day you're serving them, make a mustard sauce by mixing 130 g (4¾ oz.) wholegrain mustard, 4 tablespoons Dijon mustard and 4 tablespoons soured cream together in a saucepan and warm gently. Heat a heavy-based frying pan until it is smoking hot. Instead of using pork, rub some vegetable or groundnut oil and salt and black pepper into 450 g (1 lb.) sirloin steak. Fry the pieces of steak for 3–4 minutes each side for medium rare (depending on thickness). Rest the steak for a few minutes wrapped in aluminium foil, then slice and serve with the buns, mustard sauce and pickled kale.

CHICKEN STRIPS, PICKLED KALE AND SRIRACHA

Make the buns, kale and peanuts as per the recipe but omit the pork. Preheat the oven to 180°C/350°F/Gas Mark 4. Place 4 skinless, boneless chicken breasts between two sheets of cling film. Pound with a rolling pin until they are around 5 mm (¼ in.) thick. Sprinkle 4 tablespoons plain flour on a plate and season with salt and pepper. Crack 2 eggs into a separate dish and beat them. Sprinkle 200 g (7 oz.) dried breadcrumbs onto a third plate. Dip the chicken breasts in the flour, then the egg, and then the breadcrumbs. Pop onto greased baking trays and bake for around 30 minutes until golden brown and cooked through. Slice and serve with the buns and garnishes.

MUSHROOM, PICKLED KALE AND HOISIN

Make the buns, kale and peanuts as per the recipe. Rinse 12 large mushrooms and place in a bowl. Mix 2 tablespoons groundnut or sunflower oil with 2 tablespoons light soya sauce, 1 tablespoon black or white rice wine vinegar, 1 tablespoon minced fresh root ginger and 4 minced garlic cloves. Add to the mushrooms and turn them to coat them in the marinade. Leave them to marinate for 30 minutes. Grill the mushrooms for 10–15 minutes until they are golden brown and juicy. Slice and serve with the buns, pickled kale, peanuts and hoisin sauce.

STUFFED SWEET POTATOES WITH KALE, BLACK BEANS AND CHIPOTLE CASHEW CREAM

SERVES	4
PREP	20 minutes
COOK	1 hour 10 minutes

YOU WILL NEED

4 sweet potatoes

vegetable oil, if desired

1 tablespoon olive oil

1 onion

¼ teaspoon salt

2 garlic cloves, minced

450 g (1 lb.) cavolo nero, washed, de-stemmed and cut into thin ribbons

175 g (6 oz.) cooked black beans

175 g (6 oz.) sweetcorn kernels, thawed if frozen

FOR THE CHIPOTLE CASHEW CREAM

175 g (6 oz.) raw cashew nuts

240 ml (8 fl oz.) water

1 tinned chipotle pepper in adobo

2 garlic cloves

juice of 1 lime

½ teaspoon salt

FREE FROM DAIRY, GLUTEN & WHEAT

THESE STUFFED SWEET POTATOES ARE A DELICIOUS COMFORT FOOD PACKED WITH MAXIMUM NUTRITIONAL POWER. THEY'RE CREAMY AND DREAMY WITHOUT SACRIFICING ONE OUNCE OF HEALTHFUL VIBRANCE.

1 Preheat the oven to 200°C/400°F/Gas Mark 6.

2 To make the chipotle cashew cream, place the cashews in a food processor or liquidizer with the water, chipotle pepper, garlic, lime juice and salt. Blend for about 2 minutes, stopping to scrape down the sides as necessary, until perfectly smooth and creamy. If you're using a regular blender and any small bits of cashew remain, strain through a fine-mesh sieve if desired.

3 Scrub the sweet potatoes and dry them thoroughly. Poke some holes in various places with the tines of a fork. If you want the skins to crisp a bit, rub lightly all over with vegetable oil. Place the sweet potatoes on a foil-lined baking tray and bake for 45–75 minutes, depending on size, until tender throughout.

4 Heat the olive oil over a medium-high heat in a large frying pan. Add the onion and salt and cook for about 7 minutes, stirring from time to time, until soft. Add the garlic and cook, stirring, for 1 minute more. Add the kale and cook for about 5 minutes, stirring frequently, until wilted and tender. Stir in the beans and sweetcorn and continue to cook for about 2 minutes more, until heated through.

5 To serve, open each sweet potato, spoon on some of the kale mixture and drizzle with chipotle cream.

STUFFED SWEET POTATO VARIATIONS

KALE SHINES JUST AS BRIGHTLY ON TOP OF BAKED POTATOES. TRY A JACKET POTATO VARIATION, OR MAKE EITHER VERSION MORE FUN AND KID-FRIENDLY BY CREATING A DIY POTATO BAR.

BAKED POTATOES

Healthy baked potatoes are a must on vegetarian menus. Swap the sweet potatoes for baking potatoes. Rub the skins lightly with oil, poke some holes with the tines of a fork and place on the top shelf of a 220°C/425°F/Gas Mark 7 oven for 20 minutes. Reduce the heat to 200°C/400°F/Gas Mark 6 and cook for 40–60 minutes more, turning halfway through, until tender. For the filling, replace the black beans with chickpeas. Replace the cashew cream with soured cream.

DIY POTATO BAR

To turn this simple meal into a party, create a potato bar. Double the recipe (as required), arrange the ingredients as a buffet and let guests help themselves. You can add additional toppings like thinly sliced spring onions, and, if desired, serve the beans and sweetcorn separately from the kale to give guests more options. This also works well for kids. They're more likely to eat foods that they've helped to prepare, so get them involved in the cooking.

KALE AND SWEET POTATO BEAUTY BOWL

Rather than roasting the sweet potatoes whole, dice them into 2 cm (¾-in.) cubes. You can leave the peel on or peel them before dicing as desired. Toss with 2 tablespoons olive oil and ¼ teaspoon fine sea salt. Spread on a large baking tray or two, making sure not to crowd the pieces. Roast at 200°C/400°F/Gas Mark 6 until just tender, about 25 minutes. Toss the roasted potato pieces gently with the contents of the frying pan as per the main recipe and spoon into bowls. Drizzle with cashew cream and serve.

CASHEW CREAM

Nothing more than soaked cashews blended with a bit of water, cashew cream is a versatile dairy-free ingredient. It's an ideal base for both sweet and savoury sauces and can be used in almost any way that dairy cream can. It thickens quickly when heated and can even be whipped. The cashews pictured are roasted and salted as a snack. Use raw, untreated nuts when making cashew cream.

KALE, PARMESAN AND LEMON PEARL BARLEY RISOTTO

SERVES	4
PREP	10 minutes
COOK	35 minutes

YOU WILL NEED

1 onion, finely chopped

2 garlic cloves, finely diced

2 tablespoons olive oil

350 g (12¼ oz.) pearl barley, rinsed under cold water and drained

grated zest and juice of 1 large lemon

1.5 l (52¾ fl oz) vegetable stock

80 g (3 oz.) grated vegetarian Parmesan cheese, plus extra for serving

25 g (¾ oz.) salted butter

150 g (5¼ oz.) kale, washed, de-stemmed and shredded

salt and black pepper

FREE FROM
WHEAT

THIS TASTY RISOTTO IS MADE WITH PEARL BARLEY AND IS A LOVELY ALTERNATIVE TO THE USUAL RICE RISOTTO, AS WELL AS BEING EASIER TO COOK. SERVE WITH CRUSTY BREAD AND SALAD FOR A LIGHT LUNCH OR DINNER.

1 In a large frying pan or wok, sauté the onion and garlic in the olive oil over a low heat until soft but not brown. Add the pearl barley and cook for 2–3 minutes, stirring constantly.

2 Add the lemon zest and juice and then the vegetable stock, a ladlefull at a time, making sure it is completely absorbed before adding any more. Once the barley is soft and plump, cover the frying pan and take it off the heat. Leave to stand for 2–3 minutes.

3 Add the cheese, butter, kale and a sprinkling of salt and pepper and mix well. Return the frying pan to the heat and warm over a low heat, stirring constantly.

4 Serve in warmed bowls with extra Parmesan cheese.

PEARL BARLEY RISOTTO VARIATIONS
RISOTTO IS SUCH A COMFORTING AND POPULAR DISH, SO EXTEND YOUR RISOTTO REPERTOIRE WITH ADDED INGREDIENTS TO SUIT ALL TASTES.

BAKED BACON, KALE AND MUSHROOM RISOTTO

Why not add some crispy bacon and field mushrooms for an easy baked version of this risotto recipe? Grill 100 g (3½ oz.) chopped bacon until crisp. Soak 2 dried porcini mushrooms in 150 ml (¼ pint) boiling water for 10 minutes. Fry 100 g (3½ oz.) fresh field mushrooms in 1 tablespoon olive oil for 5 minutes until softened. Drain the porcini mushrooms, reserving the liquid, and then chop finely and add to the fried fresh mushrooms. Add the pearl barley and porcini soaking liquid and stir vigorously. Stir in the cooked bacon, 150 g (5¼ oz.) shredded kale and 450 ml (15 fl oz.) vegetable stock, then spoon it into an ovenproof dish. Cover the risotto and bake in a preheated 200°C/400°F/Gas Mark 6 oven, for 25–30 minutes, until the risotto is soft and creamy. Serve immediately with grated cheese.

MOZZARELLA-STUFFED ARANCINI

Arancini are little deep-fried rice ball fritters, usually made with leftover risotto. Place any leftovers from the original recipe into a large bowl (at least half would make about 8–10 balls). Add 50 g (1¾ oz.) breadcrumbs and 1 beaten egg to the risotto mixture. Mix well and then take handfuls of the mixture, shape into balls, and push a small cube of mozzarella cheese into the middle of each ball. Dip the balls in a beaten egg, roll in more breadcrumbs, and fry in hot oil for about 4 minutes, until golden. Drain them on kitchen towel and serve hot, sprinkled with salt and wedges of lemon.

KALE AND PEARL BARLEY-STUFFED TOMATOES

These stuffed tomatoes are easy to make and are on the table in just over half an hour. Cut 4 large tomatoes in half, spoon out the seeds, chop the remaining scooped out flesh roughly and mix with any leftover risotto. Add 1 tablespoon breadcrumbs, 50 g (1¾ oz.) grated Parmesan cheese and 2 tablespoons chopped fresh parsley or basil. Mix well and spoon the stuffing back into the tomato shells. Sprinkle a little more cheese on top and bake in a preheated 200°C/400°F/Gas Mark 6 oven, for 20–25 minutes, until the tomatoes are soft and the cheese is golden brown and melted. Serve with crusty bread and a seasonal salad.

TOMATOES

Tomatoes, whether they are fresh or tinned, count towards your five-a-day, and are packed with vitamins such as vitamin C, vitamin B6 and vitamin E. They also contain folic acid, which is essential for bone development and cell regrowth. As well as being a superfood, they can be eaten raw or cooked and are the basis of many popular family recipes. Unless you need a smooth purée, there is no need to discard the skin or the seeds.

LENTILS, CARAMELIZED ONIONS AND KALE WITH ROASTED WALNUTS

(V)

YOU WILL NEED

SERVES	4
PREP	15 minutes
COOK	20 minutes

YOU WILL NEED

200 g (7 oz.) lentils
480 ml (16 fl oz.) water
2 tablespoons olive oil
2 tablespoons (25 g) salted butter
3 onions, thinly sliced
1 teaspoon sugar
200–300 g (7–10½ oz.) kale, washed, de-stemmed and roughly chopped
crumbled blue cheese, as desired (optional)
30 g (1 oz.) chopped walnuts, roasted
salt and black pepper

FOR A SIMPLE WEEKNIGHT MEAL, ANYTHING WITH BEANS AND GREENS WINS. THIS DISH IS HEALTHY AND QUICK TO MAKE.

1 Cook the lentils in the water in a small saucepan over a medium heat. When they are tender, add I tablespoon of the olive oil and mix to help keep the lentils separated until all the water has evaporated, then remove from the heat.

2 While the lentils are cooling, place a saucepan over a medium heat and melt the butter. Add the onions, reduce the heat to low and cook for 4-5 minutes, stirring constantly as they begin to caramelize. Add the sugar, stirring until it is dissolved, then turn off the heat.

3 Put I–2 tablespoons of water in a separate saucepan, add the remaining tablespoon of olive oil and place the saucepan over a medium heat. Add the kale to the saucepan, using tongs to continuously mix and lightly steam it.

4 Add the lentils to the onions. When the water is absorbed in the saucepan of kale and the kale is cooked (you don't want it to be overcooked, just a bright green is the perfect indication it is ready), add it to the onions and lentils and mix together.

5 Pour everything into a large bowl and add the crumbled blue cheese, roasted walnuts and salt and pepper to taste.

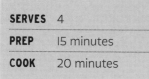

FREE FROM
GLUTEN & WHEAT

LENTIL AND KALE VARIATIONS
THESE HARICOT BEAN AND CHICKPEA VARIATIONS ARE PERFECT FOR A NIGHT WHEN YOU HAVE ZERO TIME. USE THEM TO TOP BROWN RICE OR QUINOA, OR TRY A BLACK BEAN SALAD — PERFECT FOR A SUMMER PICNIC.

KALE AND HARICOT BEAN SAUTÉ
This variation is simpler than the lentil dish but just as pleasing. Put 4 tablespoons olive oil in a saucepan over a medium heat. Add 4–6 finely minced garlic cloves and sauté for 2 minutes. Add 400 g (14 oz.) kale and continue to sauté for another 5 minutes until lightly cooked. Add I tin (400 g/14 oz.) rinsed and drained haricot beans and salt and black pepper to taste, and mix for another 5 minutes. Serve over a grain of choice and add grated cheese, if desired.

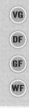

CHICKPEAS, GREENS AND TOMATOES
Similar to the white bean recipe, this one uses chickpeas instead. Add ½–I tin (200–400 g/7–14 oz.) crushed tomatoes with I tin (400 g/14 oz.) rinsed and drained chickpeas before simmering. This can be served with grains or over pasta.

KALE AND BLACK BEAN FIESTA SALAD
While the white bean variation might be better suited for a winter evening, this is a great summer dish. Put 400 g (14 oz.) kale, the juice from I lime, and I teaspoon sea salt in a large bowl. Massage the kale with your hands for 30 seconds. Add I tin (400 g/14 oz.) rinsed and drained black beans, sweetcorn kernels from I–2 ears of sweetcorn (or rinsed and drained tinned sweetcorn, or thawed frozen sweetcorn), I seeded and diced red pepper, I peeled, pitted and diced avocado, half a bunch of washed, dried and finely chopped fresh coriander and a little additional lime juice. Mix together until combined. For a non-vegan option, add I–2 tablespoons crème fraîche and stir. Add salt and black pepper to taste.

BEANS

Originating in Central and South America, beans are one of the oldest cultivated plants in the world. High in protein, fibre and magnesium, beans are a great addition to your diet if you choose to eat less meat. Try adding fresh beans to salads for a more varied texture, or add bulk to soups and stews with tins of cooked beans.

Pictured here, from top to bottom: black beans, kidney beans and mung beans.

KALE AND SWEET POTATO DOSAS WITH COCONUT CHUTNEY

(V)

SERVES	2
PREP	30 minutes
COOK	55 minutes

FOR THE DOSA BATTER

25 g (¾ oz.) chickpea (gram) flour

50 g (1¾ oz.) plain flour

½ teaspoon baking powder

½ teaspoon black mustard seeds

½ teaspoon ground turmeric

½ teaspoon garam masala

240 ml (8 fl oz.) warm water

salt

coconut oil, for frying

fresh coriander leaves and lime wedges, for serving

(continued)

FREE FROM DAIRY

DOSAS ARE SOUTHERN INDIAN PANCAKES. TRADITIONALLY MADE WITH A FERMENTED BATTER, THIS QUICK VERSION USES CHICKPEA AND PLAIN FLOUR SO YOU CAN COOK THEM IMMEDIATELY.

1 Start by making the dosa batter. Sift the flours into a bowl with the baking powder. Stir in the spices with a pinch of salt. Slowly whisk in the warm water until you have a thin batter. Put it to one side to rest while you make the chutney and filling.

2 To make the coconut chutney, warm a dry frying pan over a medium heat. Add the chana dal. Toast for 1–2 minutes until the dal smells nutty and has taken on a golden colour. Stir often while it toasts. Tip into a liquidizer or food processor.

3 Warm the coconut oil in a frying pan. Add the curry leaves and fry for 1–2 minutes until they are crisp. Add them to the chana dal with the grated coconut, chilli, ginger and cumin seeds. Add the warm water and a pinch of salt, and blend the chutney until it's smoothish. Set aside.

4 Next, make the filling. Fill a saucepan with water. Cover and bring to a boil. Add the kale and simmer without the lid for 2 minutes. Lift the kale out of the saucepan with tongs or a slotted spoon and drain in a colander. Add the chopped sweet potatoes to the saucepan. Cover and simmer for 15–20 minutes until the potatoes are tender. Poke them with a fork to check if they are done.

5 Warm the coconut oil in the frying pan you toasted the chana dal in. Add the onion and sauté over medium-low heat for 5–8 minutes until the onion is soft and a little golden. Stir in the ginger, chilli, mustard seeds and curry leaves. Cook and stir for 1–2 minutes until the mixture smells aromatic. Add the kale to the frying pan. Drain the potatoes and add them too. Stir and mash the potatoes for 2–3 minutes until they are roughly crushed. Cover and put to one side.

(continued)

FOR THE COCONUT CHUTNEY

2 tablespoons dried chana dal (or yellow split peas)

1 teaspoon coconut oil

2 teaspoons curry leaves

100 g (3½ oz.) grated fresh coconut

1 green chilli, seeded and minced

1 tablespoon fresh ginger root, minced

1 teaspoon cumin seeds

180 ml (6 fl oz.) warm water

salt

FOR THE FILLING

200 g (7 oz.) kale, washed, de-stemmed and shredded

2 sweet potatoes, peeled and chopped

1 tablespoon coconut oil

1 large onion, peeled and chopped

1 tablespoon fresh ginger root, minced

1 green chilli, seeded and minced

1 teaspoon black mustard seeds

1 tablespoon curry leaves

6 Finish the dish by frying the dosas. Wipe the frying pan clean. Melt a little coconut oil in it. Pour in a quarter of the dosa batter and swirl it round to coat the bottom of the pan so you have a thin pancake. Cook over a medium heat for 2–3 minutes – don't loosen the edges, as the batter can be very delicate.

7 When the batter is set, run a palette knife around the edges of the dosa to loosen it. Spread a quarter of the filling over the dosa. Use the palette knife to lift up one edge, then use your fingers to roll up the dosa. Slide it onto a plate to serve.

8 Repeat with the rest of the batter and potato filling to make 4 dosas. Serve them with some fresh coriander leaves and lime wedges for squeezing.

STORE CUPBOARD STAPLE: You can swap the grated fresh coconut for unsweetened desiccated coconut if you have it in your cupboard. Use 25 g (¾ oz) desiccated coconut and boiling hot water intead of warm water.

SWEET POTATOES

Sweet potatoes are super spuds. High in vitamin A, they're a good source of vitamin C and fibre. Lower in calories than white potatoes, they also count as one of your five-a-day while a regular potato doesn't. Use them when you're roasting potatoes, oven baking fries or making mashed potatoes for an extra nutritional punch along with a delicious caramel flavour.

Recipe on page 122

SOUPS, SALADS & SIDES

HEARTY FRENCH ONION AND KALE SOUP

SPICY CHICKEN AND KALE KIMCHI SOUP

POTAGE AUX LÉGUMES VERTS

SPICY MOROCCAN KALE AND RICE SOUP

KALE AND LEEK SOUP

FAMILY FAVOURITE KALE SALAD

VIETNAMESE CHICKEN SALAD

MEXICAN MASON JAR SALAD

TART CHERRY KALE SALAD WITH SMOKY DRESSING

KALE SAAG ALOO WITH HOMEMADE ROTIS

KALE GRATIN

HEARTY FRENCH ONION AND KALE SOUP

(V)

SERVES	4
PREP	15 minutes
COOK	1 hour 10 minutes

YOU WILL NEED

900 g (2 lb.) onions, sliced

2 tablespoons (25 g) salted butter

1 tablespoon olive oil

1 tablespoon fresh thyme leaves, roughly chopped

60 ml (2 fl oz.) white wine

600 ml (20 fl oz.) vegetable stock

200 g (7 oz.) kale, washed, de-stemmed and shredded

75 g (2½ oz.) grated cheddar cheese

4 slices day-old baguette

salt and black pepper

(pictured on page 120)

SHREDDED KALE ADDS FLAVOUR AND TEXTURE TO THIS NOURISHING SOUP, AS WELL AS COUNTING TOWARDS YOUR FIVE-A-DAY REQUIREMENTS. SERVED WITH TRADITIONAL CHEESE CROUTONS, IT'S A FLAVOUR-PACKED MEAL IN A BOWL.

1 Put the onions in a large stockpot with the butter, oil, and thyme, and cook over a low heat for about 45–50 minutes until the onions are sweet and caramelized.

2 Add the wine, stock and shredded kale, season to taste, and cover. Simmer over a gentle heat for 15–20 minutes until the kale is cooked.

3 Preheat the grill. Spoon the grated cheese over the tops of the baguette and grill until melted and bubbling hot.

4 For serving, ladle the soup into warmed soup bowls and top each with a cheese crouton.

SPICY CHICKEN AND KALE KIMCHI SOUP

SERVES	4
PREP	20 minutes
COOK	30 minutes

YOU WILL NEED

rapeseed or sunflower
oil, for frying

115 g (4 oz.) mixed
mushrooms, sliced

1 tablespoon fresh
ginger root, minced

2 garlic cloves, crushed

1½ tablespoons brown
miso paste

2 tablespoons mirin

1 l (35 fl oz.) water

2 boneless, skinless
chicken breasts

75 g (2½ oz.) kale kimchi
(see page 125)

1 teaspoon gochujang
(Korean red pepper
paste) or hot sauce

salt

shredded spring onions,
for serving (optional)

(pictured on page 124)

WHEREVER YOU GO IN THE WORLD, YOU'LL ALWAYS FIND CHICKEN SOUP. THIS KOREAN VERSION FEATURES SPICY KALE KIMCHI AND HOT CHILLI SAUCE TO BLOW THE COBWEBS AWAY.

1 Warm a little rapeseed or sunflower oil in a saucepan. Add the mushrooms and season with a pinch of salt. Sauté them over a medium heat for 2–3 minutes until just browned and juicy looking.

2 Stir the ginger and garlic into the mushrooms. Cook and stir for 1 minute until the saucepan smells aromatic.

3 Add the brown miso paste, mirin and water. Cover, bring to a boil, turn the heat down and add the chicken breasts to the saucepan. Simmer for 15 minutes until the chicken breasts are cooked through.

4 Lift the chicken breasts out of the stock. Let cool for a few minutes and then use two forks to shred them.

5 Add the shredded chicken to a saucepan with the kimchi and gochujang (1 teaspoon of gochujang will add some heat, so start with less if desired) and simmer for 2-3 minutes to warm through. Taste and add a little salt if needed.

6 Ladle the soup into warm bowls and scatter with a garnish of freshly shredded spring onions, if desired.

FREE FROM
DAIRY

HOW TO MAKE KALE KIMCHI

VG **DF**

KIMCHI IS A TRADITIONAL KOREAN SIDE DISH WITH A SPICY SOUR FLAVOUR. CREATED BY FERMENTING VEGETABLES IN A RANGE OF SPICES, KALE KIMCHI CAN EASILY BE MADE AT HOME.

1 Rinse 450 g (1 lb.) kale and slice it into pieces around 5 cm (2 in.) across, throwing away any thick cores. Put it in a bowl, then sprinkle with 90 g (3¼ oz.) salt and massage it into the kale. Pour enough cold water over to cover it. Cover the bowl with cling film and let sit for 24 hours at room temperature. Drain the kale and rinse it. Gently squeeze it so any excess water runs out. Return to the bowl.

2 Peel and slice 115 g (4 oz.) daikon radish into fine matchsticks. Trim and finely shred 2 spring onions. Add the daikon and spring onions to the kale with 35 g (1¼ oz.) gochugaru (Korean red pepper flakes), 4 tablespoons fish sauce, 2 tablespoons minced fresh ginger root, 3 minced garlic cloves, 1 tablespoon rice flour, 1 teaspoon Korean salted shrimp and 1 teaspoon sugar. Stir everything together until it's well mixed. Spoon the kimchi into a sterilized jar and seal and store in the fridge. After 24 hours, open it carefully to let out any gases. Put the lid back on and leave it for a week to ferment. It's best eaten within 1 month.

POTAGE AUX LÉGUMES VERTS

(V)

SERVES	6
PREP	20 minutes
COOK	30 minutes

YOU WILL NEED

4 tablespoons (50 g) butter

3 leeks, trimmed and sliced

2 garlic cloves, minced

1½ teaspoons salt

450 g (1 lb.) kale, washed, de-stemmed and shredded

1 head of broccoli, florets and stems chopped

450 g (1 lb.) baking potatoes, peeled and chopped

2 l (70 fl oz.) vegetable stock

¼ teaspoon ground nutmeg

1 dried bay leaf

a few fresh thyme sprigs

120 ml (4 fl oz.) double cream (optional), plus extra for serving

juice of ½ lemon

slices of gluten-free bread, for serving

FREE FROM
GLUTEN & WHEAT

THE SIMPLE COMFORT OF CREAMY PURÉED VEGETABLES ENRICHED WITH A BIT OF BUTTER AND CREAM IS ENOUGH TO LIFT THE SPIRITS ON EVEN THE RAINIEST AND CHILLIEST OF AFTERNOONS.

1 Melt the butter in a large saucepan. Add the leeks, garlic and salt and cook for about 5 minutes, stirring from time to time, until the leeks are beginning to be tender. Stir in the kale and cook for about 3 minutes until wilted. Stir in the broccoli and potatoes and cook for another 3 minutes.

2 Add the stock, nutmeg, bay leaf and thyme. Raise the heat to high and bring to a boil. Cover and simmer for about 20 minutes, until the vegetables are tender.

3 Remove from the heat and pick out the bay leaf and thyme stems. Using an immersion blender, carefully purée the soup until smooth. Alternatively, let the soup cool and use a liquidizer to blend in batches. Stir in the cream (if using) and lemon juice.

4 Ladle the soup into bowls and drizzle with cream (if using). Serve with warm slices of gluten-free bread, if desired.

VEGAN STYLE: To make the recipe vegan, omit the cream and replace the butter with olive oil.

POTAGE AUX LÉGUMES VARIATIONS

IT'S VERY MUCH IN THE TRADITION OF FRENCH COOKING TO ADAPT A SOUP TO THE SEASON, UTILIZING THE FRESHEST VEGETABLES AND EVEN SERVING IT CHILLED IF THE DAY CALLS FOR IT. HERE ARE SOME GREAT ALTERNATIVE OPTIONS.

ROASTED VEGETABLE SOUP

Add a more intense dimension to the flavour of your soup by roasting the broccoli. Toss with 2 tablespoons of olive oil and roast in a 200°C/400°F/Gas Mark 6 oven for about 30 minutes, turning halfway through, until browned and tender. You could even swap the broccoli for roasted cauliflower. Add the broccoli with the potatoes and proceed as in the main recipe on page 126.

SORREL SOUP

For a bright and tangy soup, add a small bunch of chopped sorrel to the soup and sauté with the kale. Omit the lemon juice.

CHILLED SOUP

In warmer months, this soup can be served chilled. Try it as an elegant garden party appetizer, or even in small glasses as a canapé.

SORREL

Technically a perennial herb, sorrel does a great job masquerading as a leafy green vegetable that's delicious shredded in salads, lightly sautéed or puréed in a smoothie. Its bright, tangy flavour adds an uplifting dimension to a wide variety of dishes.

SPICY MOROCCAN KALE AND RICE SOUP

SERVES	4
PREP	10 minutes
COOK	40 minutes

YOU WILL NEED

300 ml (10 fl oz.) vegetable stock

1 onion, diced

4 garlic cloves, minced

2 carrots, peeled and sliced

2 teaspoons ras el hanout spice mixture

½ teaspoon cayenne pepper

1 tin (400 g/14 oz.) chopped tomatoes

100 g (3½ oz.) long-grain rice

250 g (9 oz.) kale, washed, de-stemmed and shredded

salt and black pepper

crusty bread or flatbread, for serving

THIS SPICY MOROCCAN-STYLE SOUP IS LOW IN CALORIES AND FAT BUT HIGH ON FLAVOUR. PACKED WITH VEGETABLES, IT'S PERFECT FOR A LIGHT LUNCH THAT WILL LEAVE YOU SATISFIED.

1 Put a tablespoon of the stock in a large saucepan and sauté the onion, garlic and carrots for 10 minutes until softened, stirring frequently.

2 Add the spices, tomatoes, remaining vegetable stock and rice; cover and simmer for 15–20 minutes over a low heat, until the rice is cooked.

3 Season to taste with salt and pepper, add the kale, and simmer for another 5–10 minutes until the kale is cooked.

4 Serve immediately with crusty bread or warm flatbread.

FREE FROM
DAIRY, GLUTEN & WHEAT

KALE AND LEEK SOUP

(VG)

SERVES	4
PREP	15 minutes
COOK	25 minutes

YOU WILL NEED

4 tablespoons olive oil

4 leeks, trimmed and roughly sliced

½–1 head of garlic cloves, peeled and halved (this can vary depending on how much garlic you like, but use at least half a head)

chilli flakes (optional), plus extra for garnish

600 g (1 lb. 5 oz.) kale, washed and de-stemmed

960 ml (35 fl oz.) vegetable or chicken stock (recipe will not be vegan-friendly with chicken stock)

salt and black pepper

THIS SOUP IS A TOP CHOICE FOR USING FROZEN KALE. IT WORKS WELL AS A LIGHTER MEAL AND HAS A DELICIOUS, IMMUNITY-BOOSTING GARLIC KICK.

1 Pour the olive oil into a saucepan over a medium heat. Add the leeks and stir for 5 minutes. Add the garlic, ½ teaspoon of salt, a dash of pepper and a pinch of chilli flakes, if using, and continue to stir for 3 minutes. Add the kale and 250 ml (8½ fl oz.) of the stock and stir for another 5 minutes, until the kale is cooked. Add 500 ml (17 fl oz.) stock and simmer for 3–5 minutes.

2 Pour the soup into a food processor or liquidizer and blitz until smooth. Add salt and pepper to taste as needed and additional stock to thin the soup, if you like.

FREE FROM
DAIRY, GLUTEN & WHEAT

KALE SOUP VARIATIONS

TRY ADDING SOME DIFFERENT TOPPINGS TO YOUR SOUP FOR A HEARTIER DISH. A POACHED EGG ADDS ADDITIONAL CREAMINESS FROM THE YOLK, WHILE TOPPING WITH RAW FISH OR SEARED SCALLOPS TRANSFORMS THIS INTO A MAIN MEAL.

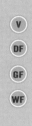

POACHED EGG AND SAUTÉED KALE

Add a poached egg and 25 g (¾ oz.) sautéed kale to the top of the soup for additional texture and flavour. Garnish with fresh parsley and/or microgreens.

(DF)

CROUTONS AND LARDONS

For a heartier version, add homemade croutons and chopped lardons. For the lardons, cut bacon into small pieces and fry in 2 tablespoons oil until well cooked. For the croutons, preheat the oven to 220°C/425°F/Gas Mark 7. Put half a baguette or 6–8 slices of day-old bread that has been cut into square, bite-size pieces into a bowl. Add 4–5 tablespoons olive oil, I teaspoon salt, some black pepper and I teaspoon garlic granules. Mix with your hands, aiming to coat every piece. Spread the bread on a baking tray covered with aluminium foil and bake for about 10 minutes, or until the bread is a golden-brown colour. Add both croutons and lardons on top of the soup.

SEARED SCALLOPS

This variation can turn the soup into more of a main plate than just a starter or lunch. Sear 2–3 scallops per person in I½ tablespoons (25 g) butter and I tablespoon olive oil with some salt and black pepper until golden brown. Add them on top of the soup with some chopped fresh parsley for garnish.

LEEKS

Including allium vegetables – bulbous plants that are members of the onion family – in your daily diet is important. Leeks, which have been cultivated in Europe for thousands of years, make a great choice because of their high quantity of vitamin K, B6 and folate. To wash, remove the thicker, dark green top and the rooted bottom and slice in half. Soak in water to remove the dirt hiding in between each layer and then prepare as required for the recipe.

FAMILY FAVOURITE KALE SALAD

(V)

SERVES	4
PREP	25 minutes
COOK	20 minutes

YOU WILL NEED

3 potatoes, cut into 1 cm (½ in.) cubes

1 tablespoon olive oil, plus 2 extra for the potato cubes

900 g (2 lb.) kale, washed and de-stemmed

1 tin (425 g/15 oz.) chickpeas, drained, rinsed and dried

35 g (1¼ oz.) pitted black Moroccan oil-cured olives, roughly chopped

1 packet (225 g/8 oz.) halloumi cheese, cut into 1 cm (½ in.) cubes

15 g (½ oz.) nutritional yeast

salt

(continued)

FREE FROM
GLUTEN & WHEAT

A GREAT WAY FOR THE WHOLE FAMILY TO EAT KALE IS TO ENJOY IT RAW IN SALADS. THIS RECIPE IS INCREDIBLY SAVOURY, AND THE BOLD FLAVOURS OF THE OLIVES, HALLOUMI AND VINAIGRETTE STAND UP WELL TO THE STRENGTH OF THE KALE.

1 First, make the vinaigrette. This recipe yields more dressing than you'll need for the kale salad – leftovers keep well in an airtight container in the fridge for up to a week and will complement a wide variety of salads, from green to bean. Combine all ingredients in a food processor or liquidizer, season with black pepper and blend until thick and creamy. Set aside until needed.

2 Preheat the oven to 220°C/425°F/Gas Mark 7.

3 Place the potato cubes on a large rimmed baking tray and toss well with 2 tablespoons of the olive oil and a generous pinch of salt. Spread the potatoes evenly over the baking tray to avoid crowding. Roast for about 20 minutes in the centre of the oven, turning with a spatula halfway through, until crisp on the outside and tender on the inside. Set aside to cool.

4 While the potatoes roast, tear the kale into small bite-size pieces. Place in a large bowl. Pour in about 60 ml (2 fl oz.) of the dressing and, using your hands, massage the dressing into the kale. This process will tenderize the kale and reduce its volume by almost half. Add the chickpeas and olives to the bowl.

(continued)

FOR THE CREAMY LEMON VINAIGRETTE

120 ml (4 fl oz.) extra-virgin olive oil

60 ml (2 fl oz.) fresh lemon juice

2 teaspoons Dijon mustard

1 garlic clove, roughly chopped

2 tablespoons nutritional yeast

½ teaspoon fine sea salt

black pepper

5 Place a medium frying pan over a medium-high heat and warm the remaining tablespoon of olive oil. Add the halloumi cubes and cook, stirring occasionally, until lightly browned on most sides and warmed through.

6 Add the cheese and potatoes to the salad bowl. Pour a little more vinaigrette onto the salad and toss all the ingredients together gently. Sprinkle on the nutritional yeast and toss once more. Serve immediately.

ADD SOME FLAVOUR: Nutritional yeast is a savoury condiment that adds a deep and satisfying umami flavour to the finished dish. It's not absolutely necessary, but you won't regret trying it.

KALE SALAD VARIATIONS
SWAPPING IN JUST A FEW INGREDIENTS CAN INTRODUCE CLASSIC FLAVOURS AND TOTALLY CHANGE THE VIBE OF THIS SALAD.

(V) (GF) (WF)

SPICY BLACK BEAN SALAD

Swap in black beans for the chickpeas and pimento-stuffed green olives for the black olives. Add a couple of diced tomatoes and 175 g (6 oz.) cooked sweetcorn kernels. In the dressing, replace half of the lemon juice with lime juice and add 1 teaspoon chilli powder or fajita seasoning before blending.

(GF) (WF)

PRAWN CAESAR

Omit the chickpeas and halloumi. In a large bowl, marinate 450 g (1 lb.) cleaned, shelled prawns in 2 tablespoons olive oil mixed with 1 tablespoon lemon juice, 2 minced garlic cloves and ¼ teaspoon salt. After 30 minutes, grill the prawns for about 2 minutes per side, until just cooked through. To the dressing, add 3 anchovy fillets. After tossing the salad, use a vegetable peeler to slice thin shavings of vegetarian Parmesan cheese over the top.

HALLOUMI

Halloumi is a Cypriot cheese made from a combination of sheep's and goat's milk. It stays intact when sautéed or grilled, so it's wonderful when cooked and then tossed into salads, cooked vegetable dishes or even sandwiches. It can be expensive, but due to its intense savouriness, a little goes a long way.

VIETNAMESE CHICKEN SALAD

SERVES	2
PREP	20 minutes
COOK	25 minutes

YOU WILL NEED

1 star anise

1 cinnamon stick

6 cardamom pods

6 black peppercorns

2 boneless, skinless
  chicken breasts

35 g (1¼ oz.) raw
  peanuts, plus extra for
  serving

200 g (7 oz.) kale,
  washed, de-stemmed
  and shredded

1 small red onion,
  thinly sliced

2 carrots, peeled and
  sliced into matchsticks

a few fresh mint sprigs,
  leaves sliced

a few fresh coriander
  sprigs, leaves diced

1 long red chilli, seeded
  and sliced

FOR THE DRESSING

juice of 1 lime

1 tablespoon light brown
  sugar

1 tablespoon rice
  wine vinegar

1 tablespoon fish sauce

1 garlic clove, minced

salt

THIS SALAD, KNOWN AS GOI GA, IS A FLAVOURFUL SPICY SALAD YOU'LL TURN TO TIME AND AGAIN.

1 Fill a deep saucepan with water. Add the star anise, cinnamon stick, cardamom pods and peppercorns. Cover and bring to a boil.

2 Slide the chicken breasts into the saucepan of boiling water. Cover, turn the heat down and simmer for 15 minutes until the chicken is cooked through. Lift the chicken out of the water and put to one side to cool. (You can keep this water for making soup – cool and store in the fridge for up to 3 days or freeze for up to 3 months. It's great for making aromatic broths.)

3 Warm a dry frying pan, add the peanuts, and toast for 1–2 minutes until they are golden and smell nutty. Keep shaking the pan so they don't burn. Turn them out onto a chopping board. Skin and roughly chop them.

4 Place the kale in a heatproof bowl. Pour in enough boiling water to cover it, leave it for 2 minutes until just softened, and then drain well.

5 Put the kale in a large bowl and add the red onion, carrots, fresh mint and coriander.

6 Shred the chicken with two forks, pulling it apart. Add to the kale.

7 Make the dressing by whisking the lime juice with the sugar, vinegar, fish sauce, garlic and a pinch of salt. Taste and add more salt if you think it needs it.

8 Add the dressing to the salad and toss to coat. Divide between 2 plates, top with the chopped peanuts and sliced chilli, and serve immediately.

FREE FROM
**DAIRY, GLUTEN
& WHEAT**

MEXICAN MASON JAR SALAD

(V)

SERVES	4
PREP	20 minutes

YOU WILL NEED

200 g (7 oz.) kale, washed, de-stemmed and shredded

2 large tomatoes, diced

1 large red onion, finely diced

pimento-stuffed green olives, cut into rings (about 6 olives per jar)

1 tin (400 g/14 oz.) red kidney beans, drained and rinsed

450 g/1 lb. salsa

6 tablespoons soured cream, mixed with 2 teaspoons Cajun seasoning

100 g (3½ oz.) grated cheese, such as cheddar

corn tortilla chips, for serving

FREE FROM GLUTEN & WHEAT

LAYERED IN A MASON (KILNER) JAR, SALAD STAYS FRESH IN THE FRIDGE OVERNIGHT AND THERE IS NO NEED FOR ANY EXTRA SALAD DRESSING. THIS ONE GETS MIXED WITH SPICY SALSA AND A SOURED CREAM TOPPING BEFORE EATING.

1 Layer the ingredients in four 1 litre (1¾ pints) mason jars in the order they are listed.

2 Place a lid on the jars and store in the fridge overnight if not eating right away.

3 Serve with corn tortilla chips for dipping.

KEEP IT FRESH: For all mason jar salads, if making the salad overnight to take to work, pour the dressing in the bottom of the jar and then layer the ingredients. For serving, shake it all up!

MASON JAR SALAD VARIATIONS
THESE HANDY AND UNIQUE RECIPE IDEAS GIVE YOU ALTERNATIVE WAYS TO ENJOY A MEAL IN A JAR WHEREVER YOU ARE.

(V)

GREEK KALE AND CHICKPEA MASON JAR SALAD
Visit the Mediterranean with this Greek-inspired salad of chopped kale layered with chickpeas, tomatoes, olives, feta cheese and cucumber in a tangy lemon dressing. Layer four 1 litre (1¾ pints) mason jars with the following ingredients, in the order listed: 200 g (7 oz.) chopped kale, 150 g (5¼ oz.) tinned chickpeas (drained), 100 g (3½ oz.) chopped cherry tomatoes, half a diced cucumber, 50 g (1¾ oz.) chopped black olives, 150 g (5¼ oz.) crumbled feta cheese. When you are ready to serve the salads, make the dressing: 2 tablespoons olive oil mixed with the juice of 1 lemon, salt, black pepper and 1 tablespoon chopped fresh oregano. You can also layer this salad in a large glass salad bowl for larger crowds – just double the quantities and serve with warmed pita chips.

(V)
(WF)
(GF)
(DF)

RAINBOW MASON JAR SALAD
This colourful rainbow salad in a jar incorporates fruits and nuts for extra crunch. Layer four 1 litre (1¾ pints) mason jars with the following ingredients, in the order listed: 200 g (7 oz.) chopped kale, 4 pink grapefruit segments (fresh or tinned), 100 g (3½ oz.) chopped almonds, 150 g (5¼ oz.) chopped strawberries, 2 chunks avocado (soaked in lemon juice), 1 tin (400 g/14 oz.) pineapple and 4 chopped tomatoes. When you are ready to serve the salad, make the dressing: 2 tablespoons honey mixed with the juice of 1 lemon and 1 tablespoon chopped fresh basil.

(V)
(WF)
(GF)

MEXICAN MASON JAR SALAD WRAPS
This recipe also makes a wonderful sandwich for a picnic, the office or a school lunchbox. Make the salad as in the main recipe on page 142, but mix all the ingredients together in a large bowl, including the salsa and Cajun soured cream. Heat 4 large corn tortillas in the microwave and spoon the filling down the middle of each tortilla – fold the two ends over and then the sides, and roll up to make a sealed wrap. Serve with extra chunky tomato salsa and salad leaves.

AVOCADOS

Smooth and delicious, avocados are very nutritious and contain more potassium than bananas. Loaded with monounsaturated fatty acids, which are great for the heart, they are also high in fibre and vitamins K, C, B5, B6 and E. Avocados do not contain any cholesterol or sodium and are low in saturated fat, making them the ideal ingredient for recipes that promote health and well-being.

TART CHERRY KALE SALAD WITH SMOKY DRESSING

SERVES 2

PREP 20 minutes

COOK 10 minutes

YOU WILL NEED

450 g (1 lb.) kale, washed, de-stemmed and chopped

3 tablespoons coconut oil

1 teaspoon tamari

1 teaspoon liquid smoke

¼ teaspoon smoked paprika

1 garlic clove, minced

5 shiitake mushrooms, sliced

½ avocado, peeled, pitted and cubed

handful of dried cherries

THIS IS A TASTY VEGAN VERSION OF THE CLASSIC SPINACH SALAD WITH BACON DRESSING.

1 Put the chopped kale in a large salad bowl. Melt the coconut oil in a frying pan over a medium heat. Stir in the tamari, liquid smoke, paprika and garlic.

2 Add the sliced mushrooms and sauté in the flavoured oil until just softened. Remove from the heat.

3 Pour the warm smoky dressing over the kale and toss to coat. Top with the avocado and cherries.

TIME-SAVING TECHNIQUE: The best way to chop kale is first to remove the tough ribs from each leaf, and then stack several leaves together and fold in half. Use a sharp knife to slice the folded kale into small strips. Repeat with the entire bunch of kale to get lots of small pieces.

LIQUID SMOKE: This product is available from several online suppliers.

FREE FROM
DAIRY, GLUTEN & WHEAT

KALE SAAG ALOO WITH HOMEMADE ROTIS

(V)

SERVES	2
PREP	30 minutes, plus resting
COOK	55 minutes

YOU WILL NEED

2 tablespoons coconut or vegetable oil

1 small onion, finely chopped

2 garlic cloves, minced

1 tablespoon fresh ginger root, minced

1 long green chilli, seeded and minced

1 teaspoon black mustard seeds

1 teaspoon cumin seeds

1 teaspoon ground turmeric

450 g (1 lb.) potatoes, peeled and chopped into small cubes

225 ml (7½ fl oz.) cold water

200 g (7 oz.) kale, washed, de-stemmed and shredded

salt and black pepper

plain natural yogurt, for serving

(continued)

SAAG ALOO IS USUALLY MADE WITH THE SPINACH IT IS NAMED AFTER, BUT ANY LEAFY GREEN IS GOOD. THIS DRY CURRY IS DELICIOUS SCOOPED UP WITH FRESH ROTIS.

1 Start by making the rotis dough (see page 150). Sift the flour into a bowl. Add in any bran that gets caught in the sieve. Sift in the baking powder then add a pinch of salt. Stir in the warm water to make a thick dough.

2 Turn the dough out onto your work surface. Knead it for 3–5 minutes until it's smooth and elastic – try not to add more flour as that will dry out the dough. Just keep kneading until it comes together.

3 Put the dough back in the bowl, cover with a clean cloth and let rest for 30 minutes.

4 Make the saag aloo. Warm the coconut or vegetable oil in a deep frying pan or wok. Add the onion and season with a little salt and pepper. Keep the heat low and fry for 5–8 minutes until the onion is soft but not coloured. If it starts to brown, turn the heat down. Keep stirring the onion as it cooks.

5 Add the garlic, ginger, chilli, mustard and cumin seeds and turmeric to the frying pan. Cook and stir for 1–2 minutes until the mixture begins to smell nutty and aromatic.

(continued)

FOR THE ROTIS

125g (4½ oz.)
   wholewheat plain flour,
   plus extra for dusting
2 teaspoons baking
   powder
60 ml (2 fl oz.) warm
   water
salt
coconut oil, for frying

6 Increase the heat to medium. Add the potatoes to the frying pan, cover with the lid, and fry for 8–10 minutes until the potatoes have picked up a little colour. Stir every so often while they cook. Add a generous 100 ml (3½ fl oz.) cold water and cook for another 10–12 minutes until the potatoes are soft.

7 Fry the rotis while the potatoes are cooking. Divide the dough into 6 pieces. Dust your work surface with a little more flour. Roll out the pieces to make rounds about 15 cm (6 in.) across.

8 Warm a teaspoon of coconut oil in a frying pan. Add one of the rotis and fry for 2–3 minutes until golden underneath. Flip and fry for another 1–2 minutes. Slide out of the frying pan into a clean cloth and loosely wrap it up (this will help keep it soft). Repeat with the rest of the rotis, adding oil to the pan as you need it.

9 Add the kale to the potatoes with another 120 ml (4 fl oz.) water. Cook and stir for 5–10 minutes until the kale has wilted and everything is cooked through. Serve the kale saag aloo with the rotis and yogurt.

SAAG ALOO VARIATIONS
WELL-SPICED GREENS HAVE A STARRING ROLE IN MANY POPULAR CURRIES. HERE ARE THREE MORE TO TRY.

GOBI SAAG ALOO
Break a head of cauliflower into small florets and spread them out on a baking tray. Drizzle with coconut oil. Roast in a preheated 180°C/350°F/Gas Mark 4 oven for 30 minutes, until they're golden brown and tender. Make the saag aloo as in the main recipe, stirring in the roast cauliflower at the end. Serves 4.

SAAG PANEER
Paneer is an unaged mild Indian cheese with a firm texture that is great for cooking. To make a creamy paneer curry, swap the potatoes for 225 g (8 oz.) paneer, cut into cubes. Add to the frying pan when you would add the potatoes and fry for 4–5 minutes until slightly coloured and warmed through. Follow the recipe but swap the water for 240 ml (8 fl oz.) coconut milk.

CHICKEN SAAG
Swap the potatoes for 2 boneless, skinless chicken breasts. Chop them into bite-size chunks and fry before the onions for 5 minutes, or until they are golden all over. Lift out of the frying pan, follow the main recipe, then add them again with the water in step 6.

KALE GRATIN

(V)

SERVES	3–4
PREP	20 minutes
COOK	45 minutes

YOU WILL NEED

1 tablespoon (15 g) butter

1–2 shallots, diced

3 garlic cloves, diced

3 large potatoes, peeled and thinly sliced

pinch of salt

pinch of ground nutmeg

300–400 ml (10½ – 13 fl oz.) whole milk

400 g (14 oz.) kale, washed, de-stemmed and roughly chopped

50 ml (1¾ fl oz.) single cream

WHILE A TRADITIONAL GRATIN RECIPE WILL USUALLY RELY ON CREAM ALONE, HERE THE KALE ADDS A NICE TEXTURE AND GREEN COLOUR ALONG WITH A WELCOME VITAMIN BOOST.

1 Preheat the oven to 200°C/400°F/Gas Mark 6. Butter a 20 cm (8 in.) baking dish or gratin dish.

2 Melt the butter in a large saucepan over a medium heat. Add the shallots and cook, stirring, for 3–4 minutes. Add the garlic and continue to stir and cook for another 2–3 minutes until soft and translucent. Add the potatoes and continue to stir and cook for 5–7 minutes.

3 Add the salt and nutmeg and cook, stirring, for 1 minute. Add the milk and cook for another 7–10 minutes. Add the kale and stir through until it wilts (this will only take about 30 seconds or so). Remove from the heat and stir in the cream.

4 Pour the mixture into the baking dish. Bake for about 30–45 minutes until the dish is bubbling and the potatoes are browned and tender.

FREE FROM
GLUTEN & WHEAT

Recipe on page 156

BAKES & DESSERTS

KALE AND MANCHEGO CHEESE SCONES

KALE, RED PEPPER AND FETA MUFFINS

KALE TART WITH AN OLIVE OIL CRUST

SAVOURY CHEESE AND KALE FLAPJACKS

ZESTY POWER BITES

TRIPLE RICH HIDDEN GEM BROWNIES

KALE AND MANCHEGO CHEESE SCONES

(V)

SERVES	6–8 scones
PREP	15 minutes
COOK	15 minutes

YOU WILL NEED

1 tablespoon butter, for greasing

180 g (6¼ oz.) self-raising flour

½ teaspoon smoked paprika

4 tablespoons (50 g) butter

125 g (4½ oz.) Manchego cheese, grated

100 g (3½ oz.) kale, washed, de-stemmed and very finely shredded

1 egg mixed with 4 tablespoons milk

salt and black pepper

butter, for serving

(pictured on page 154)

THESE CHEESE AND KALE SCONES ARE NOT ONLY WONDERFUL FOR SNACK TIME, BUT MAKE GREAT ALTERNATIVE SANDWICHES FOR THE LUNCHBOX OR TO SERVE WITH SOUPS AND STEWS.

1 Preheat the oven to 200°C/400°F/Gas Mark 6. Grease a large baking tray with a little butter.

2 Mix the flour, smoked paprika and a little salt and pepper together in a large mixing bowl and add the butter. Rub the butter into the flour mixture until it resembles fine breadcrumbs.

3 Stir in the cheese and the shredded kale and mix well.

4 Gradually add the egg and milk mixture until you have a soft dough. (Reserve a little of the egg mixture for the glaze).

5 Roll or pat the scone mixture on a floured board and shape into a large round, then cut out 6–8 rounds with a cookie cutter. Carefully place the scones onto the prepared baking tray and brush the reserved egg mixture over them.

6 Bake for 10–15 minutes, until the scones are well risen and golden brown. Leave to cool on a rack and serve warm or cold with butter.

SCONE VARIATIONS
SCONES ARE A MAINSTAY FOR MANY HOME BAKERS, AND THESE RECIPES OFFER EVEN MORE EXCITING IDEAS FOR HOW TO SERVE THEM.

KALE AND CHEDDAR SCONE SANDWICHES

Make the scones as in the main recipe, but omit the Manchego cheese and smoked paprika, and add cheddar cheese and English mustard powder instead. For serving, split the scones in half and butter both halves. Fill with your choice of sliced ham, sliced tomatoes, egg salad, sliced cucumber or your favourite savoury sandwich combination.

COBBLER TOPPING

Use this scone recipe as a savoury cobbler topping. Make the scones as in the main recipe, adding grated cheese of your choice such as vegetarian Parmesan, and then cut them into small 2.5 cm (I in.) rounds, brush them with the egg and milk mixture and sprinkle poppy seeds or sesame seeds over the top. Drop them on top of any hot (precooked) savoury stew, casserole or chilli dish and bake in a preheated oven, 200°C/400°F/Gas Mark 6, for 20 minutes until well risen and golden brown.

EGG, KALE AND CHEESE BREAKFAST SCONES

Make these scones for a leisurely weekend breakfast or brunch dish; just add eggs to order and serve with lots of freshly brewed coffee! Split the scones in half and lightly toast. Butter them and then sit freshly poached eggs on top of each half. Grind some black pepper over the eggs and offer an extra toasted scone on the side to dip into the egg yolk. Scrambled eggs are also wonderful when served this way. Or why not add some crispy fried bacon or spinach and hollandaise sauce for an eggs Florentine inspired breakfast dish?

KALE, RED PEPPER AND FETA MUFFINS

(V)

MAKES	12 muffins
PREP	15 minutes
COOK	30 minutes

YOU WILL NEED

spray oil, for greasing

1 tablespoon olive oil

2 shallots, minced

1 red pepper, finely diced

1 tablespoon chopped fresh thyme

1 tablespoon chopped fresh rosemary

½ teaspoon salt

450 g (1 lb.) cavolo nero, washed, de-stemmed and torn into bite-size pieces

125 g (4½ oz.) plain wholemeal flour

125 g (4½ oz.) plain flour

2 teaspoons baking powder

½ teaspoon bicarbonate of soda

⅛ teaspoon freshly ground black pepper

2 eggs

6 tablespoons (75 g) butter, melted

240 ml (8 fl oz.) well-shaken buttermilk

2 teaspoons Dijon mustard

115 g (4 oz.) feta cheese, crumbled

SAVOURY MUFFINS MAKE A FAMILY-FRIENDLY SNACK OR PORTABLE BREAKFAST. THIS THICK BATTER CREATES SATISFYINGLY HEARTY MUFFINS THANKS TO THE WHOLEMEAL FLOUR.

1 Preheat the oven to 200°C/400°F/Gas Mark 6 and place a rack in the centre of the oven. Coat a standard 12-cup muffin tin with spray oil or line with paper muffin cups.

2 Heat the oil over a medium-high heat in a large frying pan. Add the shallots, red pepper, thyme and rosemary, along with a sprinkle of the salt, and cook for about 5 minutes, stirring occasionally, until softened. Add the kale and cook for a further 5 minutes, stirring frequently, until it has wilted.

3 In a large mixing bowl, stir together the wholemeal flour, plain flour, baking powder, bicarbonate of soda, pepper and the remaining salt.

4 Beat the eggs, melted butter, buttermilk and mustard together with a fork in a small mixing bowl. Add to the bowl with the dry ingredients and stir gently until just combined. Fold in the contents of the frying pan and the crumbled feta cheese.

5 Divide the batter evenly among the muffin cups. Bake for about 18–20 minutes, or until a tester comes out clean. Remove from the tray and leave to cool on a rack. If using paper muffin cups, cool completely before eating so the muffins don't stick to the cups.

MIX IT UP: Feel free to play with the additions, swapping in different cheeses, herbs or vegetables, as long as the volume of ingredients remains the same.

KALE TART WITH AN OLIVE OIL CRUST

(V)

SERVES	4
PREP	30 minutes
COOK	30 minutes

YOU WILL NEED

4 tablespoons (50 g) butter

1–2 onions, thinly sliced

1 fennel bulb, fronds and base of bulb removed and thinly sliced

1–2 endive, thinly sliced

1 tablespoon fresh sage leaves, finely chopped

½ tablespoon fresh thyme

1 tablespoon sugar

200 g (7 oz.) kale, washed, de-stemmed and chopped

salt and black pepper

FOR THE OLIVE OIL CRUST

250 g (9 oz.) plain white or wholemeal flour, plus extra for dusting

pinch of sea salt

60 ml (2 fl oz.) olive oil

120 ml (4 fl oz.) water

THE SUBTLE SWEETNESS OF FENNEL AND ONIONS PAIRS NICELY WITH THE EARTHY TASTE OF KALE. TOGETHER WITH THE OLIVE OIL CRUST, THIS TART MAKES A HEALTHY AND PLEASING DISH FOR DINNER OR BRUNCH.

1 To make the crust, put the flour and salt in a mixing bowl. Create a well in the centre and pour in the olive oil. Use a fork to mix from the middle outwards until the olive oil and flour are combined as much as possible. Slowly add the water, continuing to mix, until you've used all of the liquid. Use your hands to knead the mixture in the bowl until a dough is formed.

2 Lightly dust a work surface with flour and use a rolling pin to roll out the dough to fit your tart mould (if it is not non-stick, coat with olive oil first). Place the flattened dough into the mould and remove any excess dough from the edges.

3 Preheat the oven to 200°C/400°F/Gas Mark 6.

4 Heat the butter in a saucepan over a medium heat. When the butter has melted, add the onions, fennel, endive, sage and thyme, and stir continuously as they cook. After 5 minutes, add a pinch of salt and pepper. After 10–15 minutes, stir in the sugar and cook for another 5–7 minutes.

5 Add the kale and cook for another 3 minutes until it is lightly wilted. Add another pinch of freshly ground pepper.

6 Spoon the vegetable mixture on top of the pastry and bake for 20–25 minutes until the top is crispy.

SAVOURY CHEESE AND KALE FLAPJACKS

(V)

SERVES	4–6
PREP	15 minutes
COOK	30 minutes

YOU WILL NEED

4 tablespoons (50 g) butter

100 g (3½ oz.) mixed chopped nuts, such as pecans, almonds and walnuts

150 g (5¼ oz.) kale, washed, de-stemmed and finely shredded

150 g (5¼ oz.) mature cheddar cheese, grated

125 g (4½ oz.) gluten-free rolled oats

1 teaspoon fresh thyme

1 egg, beaten

½ teaspoon cayenne pepper

salt and freshly ground black pepper

THESE CHEESE AND KALE OAT FLAPJACKS ARE VERY TASTY AND EASY TO MAKE; A SAVOURY TAKE ON THE USUAL SWEET RECIPE, THEY ARE GREAT FOR LUNCHBOX SNACKS AS WELL AS PICNICS.

1 Preheat the oven to 180°C/350°F/Gas Mark 4. Grease and line a 27 x 15 cm (11 x 7 in.) baking tray.

2 Melt the butter and stir in the mixed nuts, shredded kale, grated cheese, oats, thyme and beaten egg, and mix well. Season with cayenne pepper, salt and pepper to taste, and mix well.

3 Spoon into the prepared tray. Press down and bake for 25–30 minutes, or until golden brown.

4 Leave to cool in the tray and then divide into bars or squares. Store in an airtight tin or container for up to 1 week.

FREE FROM
GLUTEN & WHEAT

OATS

Oats have long been associated with a healthy diet and have many nutritional benefits for the whole family; they are loaded with dietary fibre (containing more than any other grain) and have a range of healthy cholesterol-lowering properties. In addition to being a breakfast staple, oats make a fabulous added ingredient in pastry, bakes, dumplings and scones, and are a great thickening agent in soups and stews. Research shows that eating just three servings of whole grains a day, such as oats, may help to reduce the risk of heart disease by up to 30 per cent as part of a healthy diet and lifestyle.

ZESTY POWER BITES

MAKES	10–12 bites
PREP	15 minutes

YOU WILL NEED

195 g (6¾ oz.) raw cashew nuts

10 dried dates, pitted

70 g (2½ oz.) kale, washed, de-stemmed and finely chopped

juice and grated zest of 1 lemon, about 60 ml (2 fl oz.)

THESE SUPER QUICK BITES MAY ATTRACT SOME ODD LOOKS BECAUSE OF THE GREEN COLOUR, BUT THE LEMONY SWEET FLAVOUR WILL KEEP PEOPLE COMING BACK FOR MORE.

1 Pulse the cashews into small pieces in a food processor or liquidizer. Add the dates and pulse again to combine.

2 Add the kale, lemon juice and zest, and pulse once more until combined.

3 Roll the mixture into golf ball-size bites. Store, covered, in the fridge for 7–10 days.

FREE FROM
DAIRY, GLUTEN & WHEAT

TRIPLE RICH HIDDEN GEM BROWNIES

(VG)

MAKES	12
PREP	15 minutes
COOK	35 minutes

YOU WILL NEED

spray oil, for greasing

2 tablespoons freshly ground flaxseed

80 ml (2¾ fl oz.) warm water

100 g (3½ oz.) gluten-free plain flour

150 g (5¼ oz.) sugar

65 g (2½ oz.) vegan cocoa powder

½ teaspoon bicarbonate of soda

½ teaspoon sea salt

50 g (1¾ oz.) kale, washed and de-stemmed

120 g (4 oz.) vegan chocolate almond milk

120 g (4 oz.) vegan dark chocolate, chopped

100 g (3½ oz.) coconut oil

55 g (2 oz.) dark vegan chocolate chips, for topping

FREE FROM
DAIRY, GLUTEN
& WHEAT

NOBODY WILL BE ABLE TO DETECT THE HIDDEN GEM IN THESE BROWNIES — WHICH IS A NICE DOSE OF GREENS!

1 Preheat the oven to 180°C/350°F/Gas Mark 4 and line a 20 x 20 cm (8 x 8 in.) square baking tin with baking paper and coat with oil.

2 Place the ground flaxseed in a bowl, add the warm water, and stir. Refrigerate for 10-15 minutes until it forms a gel (this is the equivalent of adding 2 eggs).

3 Sift together the flour, sugar, cocoa, bicarbonate of soda and sea salt in a large mixing bowl and set aside.

4 Combine the kale and chocolate almond milk in a food processor or liquidizer and blitz on the highest speed to a liquid. Set aside.

5 Melt the chopped chocolate and coconut oil in a small saucepan set over a low heat. Remove from the heat when completely melted and set aside to cool.

6 Pour the kale liquid and flaxseed gel into the melted chocolate and stir to combine. Add this chocolate mixture to the dry ingredients, stirring to combine completely.

7 Pour the brownie batter into the prepared baking tin and sprinkle the surface with chocolate chips. Bake for 30 minutes, or until a toothpick or skewer inserted in the centre comes out clean.

GRIND YOUR OWN: Most high-speed liquidizers will allow you to grind your own flaxseed, but you can use a coffee grinder. Alternatively, you can use ready-ground flaxseed.

KALE BROWNIE VARIATIONS

SWIRLING NUT BUTTER INTO A BROWNIE OR ADDING RICH AND SWEET CREAM CHEESE MAKES THESE BROWNIES EXTRA DECADENT. ADDING A TART BITE OF FRUIT OR CRUNCHY MIXED NUTS AND SWEETS ELEVATES THEM EVEN HIGHER!

(VG) (GF) (WF)

ALMOND BUTTER SWIRL BROWNIES

Combine 75 g (2½ oz.) almond butter, 2 tablespoons chopped dry-roasted almonds and 2 tablespoons sugar in a bowl. Swirl into the top of the brownies (made following the instructions for the main recipe) before baking.

(VG) (GF) (WF)

TRAIL MIX BROWNIES

Stir 55 g (2 oz.) salted peanuts, 55 g (2 oz.) mixed dried fruit, 40 g (1½ oz.) vegan sugar-coated chocolate chips and 30 g (1 oz.) chopped walnuts into the brownie batter (made following the instructions for the main recipe) before baking.

(VG) (GF) (WF)

CHERRY CHEESECAKE BROWNIES

Combine 120 g (4 oz.) dairy-free cream cheese, 30 g (1 oz) chopped dried cherries and 2 tablespoons sugar in a bowl. Swirl into the top of the brownies (made following the instructions for the main recipe) before baking.

DARK CHOCOLATE

Dark chocolate just might be everyone's favourite superfood – rich, sweet and satisfying. A good quality chocolate is loaded with antioxidants, minerals and fibre, in addition to an incredibly rich flavour and mood-enhancing serotonin boost. A square a day will keep you quite happy – melt it into your breakfast porridge, blend it into your workout recovery smoothie, drizzle it over a bowl of fresh fruit or enjoy it in a delectable kale brownie!

INDEX

RECIPE LIST BY BLOGGER

32

46

28

40

54

82

43

109

 26

 71

 85

 92

 104

 126

136

158

CAROLYN COPE

62

68

76

88

98

101

117

148

JASSY DAVIS

22

35

58

72

91

97

164

167

KRISTINA SLOGGETT

ACKNOWLEDGEMENTS

Thank you so much to Kristen Beddard who wrote the fantastic introduction to this book (pages 10-19).

Many thanks to Discoverkale.co.uk for supplying all the wonderful kale for the recipes in this book.

Thanks to Abi Waters, Anna Southgate, Rachel Malig and Ann Barrett.

Quantum Books would like to thank the following for supplying images for inclusion in this book:

Istock.com: MonaMakela 11; **Shutterstock.com**: AnjelikaGr 8-9; Mandy Godbehear 12; Zigzag Mountain Art 17; Coconut 25; Es75 30; Marysckin 39; Andreja Donkox 49; Jiri Hera 61, 145; Marylooo 74; Wiktory 83; GooDween123 94; Brian Zanchi 106; Shebeko 111; Amarita 115; Exopixel 118; Antonova Anna 128; Gorenkova Evgenija 134; Tom Gowanlock 138; Africa Studio 168.

While every effort has been made to credit contributors, Quantum Books would like to apologize should there have been any omissions or errors and would be pleased to make the appropriate correction to future editions of the book.